© Copyright 1995
All Rights Reserved
Revised Edition 2007

Library of Congress Catalog Card Number: 96-83109
ISBN: 0-911119-71-X

Family Values In Islam

By

Ahmad H. Sakr, Ph.D.

Published by:
Foundation for Islamic Knowledge
P.O. Box 665
Lombard, Illinois 60148 (USA)
Telephone: (630) 495-4817
FAX: (630) 627-8894
Tax I.D #36-377-4566
E-mail ahmadsakr@yahoo.com
Website: www.ahmadsakr.com

NOTE: Your generous contribution to this **Foundation** will enable us to publish more valuable literature and to render more services to all. The **Foundation** has a tax-exempt status with the IRS. Your donations are tax-deductible.

i

Family Values In Islam

Table Of Contents

The name of the Prophet Muhammad
In mirror images,

iii

Dedication

God's Majesty Exalted

This book is dedicated to Allah Ta'ala (Almighty) for all the favors He has bestowed upon me in creating and bringing me to this world. His Love, His Mercy, His Compassion, His Forgiveness, His Graciousness, His Kindness and His Bountifulness are above any humble person like me, to be able to thank Him enough and to praise Him.

O Allah!   I am humbly dedicating this work **to You.**

O Allah!   Accept my humble work and help me disseminate the information to those who need it.

O Allah!   Make this humble work worthy **of You.**

O Allah!   Forgive my shortcomings.

O Allah!   Help me live as a Muslim and die as a Mu'min (Believer).

O Allah!   Let me be summoned on the Day of Judgment with Prophet Muhammad (pbuh), with the other Prophets, the martyrs and all the noble believers. Ameen.

Acknowledgements

- Special thanks go to Dr. and Mrs. Mohammad Shafi and their family, as well as to the Al-Qur'an Foundation of Milwaukee, Wisconsin for their tremendous help in publishing the First Edition of this book. The author is very thankful to them. May Allah bless them and reward them.

- The author wishes to thank all those friends who helped him in making this book and the previous books available to the readers. Special thanks go to Dr. Yusuf Kamaluddin (Yao-Keng) Chang and his wife, Audrey, for their tremendous help and moral support during the last few years. Thanks and appreciations go to the Vakil families (Abu Bakr, Usman, Farouq, Ishaq, Iqbal, and Akhtar) for their support to the author and the Foundation. May Allah (swt) bless them and bless their late parents (Umar and Amina). Thanks and appreciations go to Dr. and Mrs. Ahmed K. Noor for taking care of the Newsletter: **Perspectives** for a number of years and from their own personal expenses.

- Moreover, the author wishes to thank all the respected brothers and sisters who have helped previously and are still helping. Among the many are Mr. Asad Khan and his wife, Sister Azma Khan; Dr. and Mrs. Mohammed Shafi; Mr. & Mrs. Javed Habib; Mr. & Mrs. Abdul Wahab; Mr. & Mrs. Saghir Aslam; Dr. & Mrs. Nadim Daouk; Mr. Refat M. Abo Elela; Dr. & Mrs. Zeyd A. Merenkov; Dr. and Mrs. Daudur Rahman; Mr. and Mrs. Shakeel Syed; Dr. and Mrs. Maqbool Ahmad; Mr. Zia Khan and his wife Tina Khan; Dr. and Mrs. Syed A. Zahir; Dr. and Mrs. Muhammad K. Zaman; Dr. and Mrs. Mostapha Arafa; Dr. & Mrs. Samir Arafeh; Dr. M. Munir Chaudry and his family; the late Dr. F.R. Khan and his respected wife Sister Farhat Khan, may Allah (swt) bless his soul, and many more.

- Thanks and appreciation goes to Dr. Dany Doueiri for translating some chapters from Arabic to English, as well as typing the Arabic texts and index of some books. May Allah bless him and reward him and his family. Ameen.

• Special thanks and appreciations go to Sister Fawzia Akalal; Sister Sajeda Sultani and her family; Sister Houyda Najjar Mertaban and her family; Brother Mohammed Bilal Khan and his family; and Brother Waseem Najmi and his wife Yasmeen for their kind help in many areas. Also our thanks and appreciation is extended to Sister Azizah Abdul Rahman of Singapore, on behalf of her late parents Aminah Bint Ahmad and Abdul Rahman bin Mohamed. May Allah (swt) be pleased with her and her late parents. Ameen.

• Special thanks and appreciations go to Sister Shadia Hassan and her children for their help, advice, and contributions for the love of Allah (swt). Our prayers of Maghfirah for her late husband Mr. Samir Hassan and her late father Mr. Ahmad Ali. May Allah (swt) bless their souls and make their final stay in Paradise. Ameen. We are thankful and grateful to Mr. Muhammad El-Bdeiwi and his family for their generosity in helping this Foundation for Da'wah purposes. Our thanks also go to Mr. & Mrs. Abu Ramy Assaf, as well as to Dr. Yusuf K. Deshmukh and his family. Our thanks and appreciations go to Mr. Ammar Charani and his brother Samer Charani of Muslim Education Funds (MEF) for their help. May Allah (swt) bless them all. Our thanks go to Mr. Anwar Haq and his wife Blanca Haq and family members for their moral support to this Foundation.

• Thanks and appreciations go to Mr. Khaled Obagi for his support to the Foundation on behalf of his late father and mother Aref Obagi and Nabila Al-Beik. Our thanks and appreciations also go to Mr. Ahmad Al-Khatib for his support to the Foundation on behalf of his mother Soraya, and his late father Adel Baheej Al-Khatib. Thanks and appreciation also goes to Dr. Osama Haikal on behalf of his late father, Mr. Omar Haikal. May Allah (swt) be pleased with them and may Allah (swt) keep their relatives in Paradise. Ameen. Our thanks and affections go to Brother Fathy Haggag and his family for their tremendous support to the author for all the years in California. It is only Allah (swt) Who will reward them. Our heartfelt thank to my brother, Samir and his family for their excellent management of this Foundation. Thanks and appreciations go to Abu Firas and Umm Firas Meher as well as Br. Ali Al-Najjar for their support of the Masjid (IEC) and Da'wah through literature.

• Thanks and appreciations go also to Dr. Muhammad Waleed Khalife and his family for their support to this Foundation. May Allah (swt) bless them and reward them. Moreover, our thanks and appreciation go to Dr. Syed A. Rizvi and his family for their personal help to the author and to this Foundation. May Allah bless them and reward them. Ameen.

• Thanks and appreciations are to Mr. Kamel Daouk and his brothers who helped this Foundation by supplying papers for printing the books. Yes Indeed! we are thankful and grateful to Brother Hassan Igram who is the president of Cedar Graphics Company, and who has been helping this Foundation for the last 25 years by printing most of the books. Moreover, we are thankful to Mr. Anwer Khan and his brothers of A-1 Printing and Graphics who helped this Foundation by printing a good number of pamphlets. May Allah (swt) bless all of them. Ameen. We are thankful to Brother Talal Smadi who contributed the Arabic typesetting for this Book and previous ones. May Allah (swt) bless him and reward him in this world and in the Hereafter.

• Last but not least, my thanks, appreciation and love are to my wife, Zuhar Barhumi Sakr and our loving children: Sara and her husband Mohamad Nasser and their children Nada, Abdul Rahman, Ibrahim, Jenna, Hannah, Amber, Sabrina and Adam; to Hussein and his wife Dania and daughters Ayah and Dana; to Jihad and his wife Nasrin, son Hamza and daughters Sumaiya and Sawsan; to Basil and his wife La Reina and daughters Amina, Randa, and Yasmine. *We pray to Allah (swt) to open the hearts of other friends to invest with Allah (swt)*

Special Prayers

- The author prays to Allah (swt) to bless Prophet Muhammad and the family of Prophet Muhammad (pbuh), in as much as He blessed Prophet Ibrahim and the family of Prophet Ibrahim (pbuh). The author also prays to Allah (swt) to bless the Khulafaa' Rashidoon (Rightly guided) and the Sahaba (Companions) of the Prophet (pbuh) as well as the Tabi'oon (Followers) and the Followers of the Followers till the Day of Judgment.

- The author prays to Allah (swt) to reward all the 'Ulama', who carried the Message of Allah (swt) and His Prophet (pbuh), and who transmitted it to the new generations.

- The author prays to Allah (swt) to reward his parents: his late father Al-Hajj Hussain Mustafa Sakr and his late mother Al-Hajjah Sara Ramadan Sakr for their sacrifices on their twelve children in general and to this author in specific. The author prays to Allah (swt) to reward the late brother of the author, Mr. Muhammad H. Sakr, for helping the author get his academic education, and his late brothers Mahmood H. Sakr, and Mustafa H. Sakr for taking care of the author's responsibilities overseas.

- Special prayers go to the Shaikh of the author who taught him Islam, and trained him from childhood to practice its teachings: Shaikh Muhammad 'Umar Da'ooq. May Allah (swt) be pleased with him.

- A special Du'aa' goes to Al-Shaheed Shaikh Hassan Khalid, the late Grand Mufti of Lebanon, who also had a great impact on the author's knowledge of Islam. May Allah (swt) bless his soul and grant him a place in Paradise.

---

1. swt: Subhanahu Wa Ta'ala (Glory be to Allah, and He is The High).
2. pbuh: Peace Be Upon Him (The Prophet).

- Special prayers and Du`aa' go to the many teachers, scholars and `Ulamaa' who were directly tutoring this author at the time of his youth. Through the efforts of Shaikh Muhammad `Umar Da'ooq, the following is a partial list of the teachers who taught this author: Dr. Mustafa Siba`ee; Shaikh Muhammad M. Al-Sawwaf; Dr. Muhammad Al-Zo`by; Shaikh Muhammad `Itani; Shaikh Muhammad M. Da`ooq; Shaikh Al-Fudail Al-Wartalani; Shaikh Muhammad `Abdel Kareem Al-Khattabi; Shaikh Malik Bennabi; Shaikh Faheem Abu`Ubeyh; Shaikh Muhammad Al-Shaal; Dr. Sa`eed Ramadan; Attorney `Abdel Hakeem `Abideen; Dr. Tawfic Houri; Shaikh Abu Salih Itani; Shaikh Hashim Daftardar Al-Madani; and the late Shaikh Abdul Badee` Sakr. May Allah (swt) bless them and reward them all.

- Our thanks and appreciation goes to Dr. M. Faseehuddin and all his family members for their contribution to this Foundation. A special thanks and appreciation go to Sister Dr. Sayeeda Sultana for donating on behalf of her mother, Mrs. Sultany Begum. May Allah (swt) reward Dr. Sultana, and may Allah (swt) bless her mother Sultany Begum. Moreover, we do thank Mr. and Mrs. Haitham Bundakji for their generosity to this Foundation at the time of needs. Ameen. Special thanks and appreciation go to Mr. Talat Radwan for helping this Foundation on behalf of his late father Mr. Mahmoud Radwan. May Allah (swt) bless them and be pleased with them both. Moreover, we do thank Dr. M.F. Shoukfeh, M.D. and his family for their generous help to this Foundation.

- A final prayer is to the readers who took their precious time in reading this humble Book **Family Values In Islam**. May Allah (swt) bless them all. Allahumma Ameen.

Supplications

O Allah ! I seek refuge **in You** from anxiety and grief...
I seek refuge **in You** from incapacity and laziness.. and
I seek refuge **in You** from the overcoming of debts and
overpower of people...

O Allah ! I seek refuge **in You** from poverty except **to You,**...
from humiliation except **for You,** and from fear except
from You.

O Allah ! I seek refuge **in You** from stating false testimony... or
committing immorality, or provoking **You**; and
I seek refuge **in You** from the malice of the enemies,
and from enigmatic disease, and from the despair of
hope.

O Allah ! I seek refuge **in You** from the wicked people... from
the worries of the livelihood, and from the ill-nature..

O Allah ! **You are** the Mercy of the mercies, and **You are** the
Lord of the Universe.

Ya Allah!
Allahumma Ameen.

Supplications

بِسْمِ اللهِ الرَّحْمٰنِ الرَّحِيمِ

اللّٰهُمَّ

اللَّهُمَّ إِنِّى أَعُوذُ بِكَ مِنَ الْهَمِّ وَالْحَزَنِ
وَأَعُوذُ بِكَ مِنَ الْعَجْزِ وَالْكَسَلِ
وَأَعُوذُ بِكَ مِنْ غَلَبَةِ الدَّيْنِ وَقَهْرِ الرِّجَالِ
اللَّهُمَّ إِنِّى أَعُوذُ بِكَ مِنَ الْفَقْرِ إِلَّا إِلَيْكَ
وَمِنَ الذُّلِّ إِلَّا لَكَ وَمِنَ الْخَوْفِ إِلَّا مِنْكَ
وَأَعُوذُ بِكَ أَنْ أَقُولَ زُورًا أَوْ أَغْشَى فُجُورًا
أَوْ أَكُونَ بِكَ مَغْرُورًا وَأَعُوذُ بِكَ
مِنْ شَمَاتَةِ الْأَعْدَاءِ وَعُضَالِ الدَّاءِ
وَخَيْبَةِ الرَّجَاءِ اللَّهُمَّ إِنِّى أَعُوذُ بِكَ
مِنْ شَرِّ الْخَلْقِ وَهَمِّ الرِّزْقِ وَسُوْءِ الْخُلُقِ
يَا أَرْحَمَ الرَّاحِمِينَ وَيَا رَبَّ الْعَالَمِينَ

xi

INTRODUCTION

The title of this book is Family Values in Islam. Family is the cornerstone and the foundation for a society. If and when a family is built on solid and stable foundation, then the society will be solid and stable as well. A family is considered a family when it is composed of its integral components, and when it is based on duties and responsibilities.

The integral components are: husband; wife; children; grandparents from both husband and wife; uncles, aunts, cousins, nephews and nieces from both sides of husband and wife; and many more. All of these constitute a family with rules and regulations, as well as with duties and responsibilities. As far as duties and responsibilities are concerned, they are related to marriage; divorce; khul'ah; custody; inheritance; fostering (not adoption); burial; zakat, charity, family counselling; and so on.

This particular book cannot deal with all these subjects in one document. However, this book deals with the following subjects: Family in Islam, Khutbatun Nikah, Contraception, Parent & Children Relationships, Family Problems: Causes and Solutions, UN Conference 1994 on Population and Development, Adoption and Fostering, Current Issues of Halal Foods, Choosing Wrong Food Products, Food and Overpopulation, Food of Heaven and Hell, Securing an Easy Divorce, Islamic Arbitration, A Sudden Tragedy in the Family, Neighbors, Respect of

Parents, The Elderly, Orphans, A Message of Condolence; other related materials.

It should be stated here that Chapter three (3) about contraception has been written by both the author and Dr. Mohammad Shafi, M.D., F.A.C.O.G. They presented the medical and religious aspects of family planning as well as birth control.

This book is among the series of books that Al-Quran Foundation of Milwaukee under the leadership of Dr. Mohammad Shafi, M.D., has agreed to help the Foundation for Islamic Knowledge of Illinois to publish. It is the hope and wish of the author that some more individuals, groups, organizations or foundations would come forward to sponsor any of the literature to be published and distributed. The door is open to all and we hope that someone will come forward to sponsor some of the following books to be published in the future 'Insha Allah:

Islamic Understanding, The Book of Healing, The Book of Targheeb, The Book of Inquiries, Death and Dying, The Flying Falcon Speaks, Islamic Shari'ah Textbook, The Adolescent Life, Health, Hygiene and Nutrition, Halal/Haram Book of Khutab, Speakers' Bureau Guide Book, etc.

We hope and pray that Allah will accept from all of us what has been done, and forgive us for our shortcomings. Allahumma Ameen.

"There is no god but Allah and Muhammad is the Messenger of Allah"

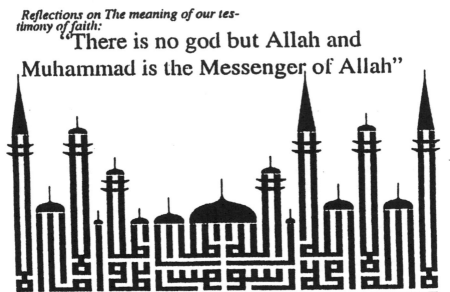

An-Nisāa, or The Women.

In the name of Allah, Most Gracious
Most Merciful.

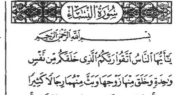

1. O mankind! fear
   Your Guardian Lord,
   Who created you
   From a single Person,[504]
   Created, out of it,
   His mate, and from them twain
   Scattered (like seeds)
   Countless men and women;–
   Fear Allah, through Whom[505]
   Ye demand your mutual (rights),
   And be heedful of the wombs[506]
   (That bore you): for Allah
   Ever watches over you.

2. To orphans restore their property
   (When they reach their age),
   Nor substitute (your) worthless things
   For (their) good ones; and devour not

   Their substance (by mixing it up)[507]
   With your own. For this is
   Indeed a great sin.

3. If ye fear that ye shall not
   Be able to deal justly
   With the orphans,[508]
   Marry women of your choice,
   Two, or three, or four;
   But if ye fear that ye shall not
   Be able to deal justly (with them),
   Then only one, or
   That which your right hands possess.
   That will be more suitable,
   To prevent you
   From doing injustice.[509]

4. And give the women
   (On marriage) their dower
   As an obligation; but if they,
   Of their own good pleasure,
   Remit any part of it to you,
   Take it and enjoy it
   With right good cheer.

1

Chapter 1
FAMILY IN ISLAM

I. DEFINITION OF A FAMILY

A. A group comprising the immediate kindred, especially the group formed by parents and children.

B. Those descended from a common progeny: a tribe, a clan, or a kindred race.

II. COMPOSITION OF A FAMILY

In Western societies, the composition of a family is mainly made up of a husband, a wife, and their immediate children. According to Muslim teachings, the composition of a family includes the following:

A. Husband, wife and children;

B. Grandchildren;

C. Parents of the husband and wife;

D. Brothers and sisters of both husband and wife;

E. Uncles and aunts from both husband and wife; and,

F. Nephews and nieces from both husband and wife.

Such a composition, as above, is considered in the Western societies to be the extended family. In this regard, the Qur'an states in Surah Al-Nahl (The Bees) the following:

وَٱللَّهُ جَعَلَ لَكُم مِّنْ أَنفُسِكُمْ أَزْوَٰجًا وَجَعَلَ لَكُم مِّنْ أَزْوَٰجِكُم بَنِينَ وَحَفَدَةً وَرَزَقَكُم مِّنَ ٱلطَّيِّبَٰتِ أَفَبِٱلْبَٰطِلِ يُؤْمِنُونَ وَبِنِعْمَتِ ٱللَّهِ هُمْ يَكْفُرُونَ ﴿٧٢﴾

And Allah has given you wives of your own kind, and has given you from your wives, sons and grandsons, and has made provision of good things for you. Is it then in vanity that they believe and in the grace of Allah that they disbelieve? **(16:72)**

This type of a family composition is referred to in the Qur'an to be of any of the following:

A. ʿAshirah. This word is used in the Qur'an four times in different ways and forms.

B. Arham. This word is found six times in the Qur'an.

C. Qurba, Al-Aqraboon or Al-Aqrabeen. These terms are mentioned eleven times in the Qur'an.

D. 'Aa'il. This word is used three times in the Qur'an.

E. Nasab/Ansab. These words are found in the Qur'an three times.

As far as the word ʿashirah is concerned, the Qur'an states in Surah Al-Shu'ara' (The poets) the following:

وَأَنذِرْ عَشِيرَتَكَ ٱلْأَقْرَبِينَ ﴿٢١٤﴾

4

And warn your tribe ('Ashirah) of near kindred.
(26:214)

Also, Allah says in the Qur'an in Surah Al-Tawbah
(Repentance) the following:

قُلْ إِن
كَانَ ءَابَآؤُكُمۡ وَأَبۡنَآؤُكُمۡ وَإِخۡوَٰنُكُمۡ وَأَزۡوَٰجُكُمۡ وَعَشِيرَتُكُمۡ
وَأَمۡوَٰلٌ ٱقۡتَرَفۡتُمُوهَا وَتِجَٰرَةٌ تَخۡشَوۡنَ كَسَادَهَا وَمَسَٰكِنُ
تَرۡضَوۡنَهَآ أَحَبَّ إِلَيۡكُم مِّنَ ٱللَّهِ وَرَسُولِهِۦ وَجِهَادٍ
فِى سَبِيلِهِۦ فَتَرَبَّصُوا۟ حَتَّىٰ يَأۡتِىَ ٱللَّهُ بِأَمۡرِهِۦ وَٱللَّهُ لَا يَهۡدِى
ٱلۡقَوۡمَ ٱلۡفَٰسِقِينَ ﴿٢٤﴾

Say: If your fathers, and your sons, and your
brothers, and your wives, and your tribe
('Ashirah), and the wealth you have acquired,
and merchandise for which you fear that there
will be no sale, and dwellings you desire are
dearer to you than Allah and His Messenger and
striving in His way: then wait till Allah brings
His command to pass. Allah guides not wrong-
doing folk.
(9:24)

The word 'Ashirah is also mentioned in Surah Al-Mujadalah
(She That Disputes) as follows:

5

لَّا تَجِدُ قَوْمًا يُؤْمِنُونَ بِاللَّهِ وَالْيَوْمِ الْأَخِرِ يُوَآدُّونَ مَنْ
حَآدَّ اللَّهَ وَرَسُولَهُ وَلَوْ كَانُوٓاْ ءَابَآءَهُمْ أَوْ أَبْنَآءَهُمْ
أَوْ إِخْوَانَهُمْ أَوْ عَشِيرَتَهُمْ أُوْلَٰٓئِكَ كَتَبَ فِي قُلُوبِهِمُ
الْإِيمَانَ وَأَيَّدَهُم بِرُوحٍ مِّنْهُ وَيُدْخِلُهُمْ جَنَّاتٍ تَجْرِي
مِن تَحْتِهَا الْأَنْهَارُ خَالِدِينَ فِيهَا رَضِيَ اللَّهُ عَنْهُمْ وَرَضُواْ
عَنْهُ أُوْلَٰٓئِكَ حِزْبُ اللَّهِ أَلَآ إِنَّ حِزْبَ اللَّهِ هُمُ الْمُفْلِحُونَ ۝

You will not find folk who believe in Allah and the Last Day loving those who oppose Allah and His Messenger, even though they be their fathers or their sons or their brothers or their clan. As for such, He has written faith upon their hearts and has strengthened them with a Spirit from Him, and He will bring them into Gardens underneath which rivers flow, wherein they will abide. Allah is well pleased with them, and they are well pleased with Him. They are Allah's party. Lo! is it not Allah's party who are the successful?

(58:22)

As far as the category of Arham (kins and kiths) is concerned, the Qur'an states in Surah Al-Anfal (Spoils of War) the following:

وَالَّذِينَ ءَامَنُواْ مِنۢ
بَعْدُ وَهَاجَرُواْ وَجَٰهَدُواْ مَعَكُمْ فَأُوْلَٰٓئِكَ مِنكُمْ وَأُوْلُواْ الْأَرْحَامِ
بَعْضُهُمْ أَوْلَىٰ بِبَعْضٍ فِي كِتَٰبِ اللَّهِ إِنَّ اللَّهَ بِكُلِّ شَيْءٍ عَلِيمٌ ۝

6

And those who afterwards believed and left their homes and strove along with you, they are of you; and those who are akin are nearer one to another in the ordinance of Allah. Lo! Allah is Knower of all things. (8:75)

The Qur'an also states in Surah Al-Ahzab (The Clans) the following about Arham:

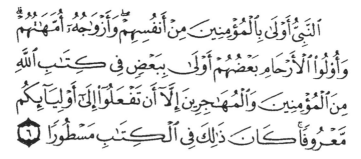

The Prophet is closer to the believers than their ownselves, and his wives are (as) their mothers. And the owners of kinship are closer one to another in the ordinance of Allah than (other) believers and the fugitives (who fled from Makkah), except that you should do kindness to your friends. This is written in the Book of Allah.

(33:6)

One may read in Surah Al-Mumtahanah (She That Is To Be Examined) the following about Arham:

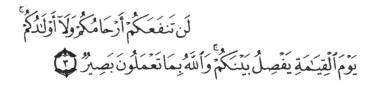

Your ties of kindred and your children will avail you naught upon the Day of Resurrection. He will part you. Allah is Seer of what you do. **(60:3)**

On may also read the following about Arham in Surah Muhammad:

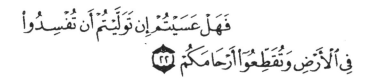

Would you then, if you were given the command, work corruption in the land and sever your ties of kinship? **(47:22)**

III. CONTEMPORARY FAMILY PROBLEMS

There are many problems related to families. They are too many to be recorded; however, a partial list is mentioned in this article. They are subdivided as follows:

A. Husband-Wife Relations

Some of the major contemporary problems related to this area are:

1. Separation or divorce

2. Extra-marital relations

3. Battered wives by husbands

4. Drugs and alcohol abuse

5. Leaving wives with children to go on welfare and public aid, and;

6. Family counseling

B. Parent-Child Relationship

Some of the major problems facing this group are the following:

1. Abused children by parents

2. Child neglect: leaving children to be taken care of by:

   a. Other children

   b. Baby sitters

   c. Television

3. Children born out of wedlock.

4. Children being kidnapped by one parent or the other:

a. As a matter of love for the children, or

b. Out of revenge for the other parent.

5. Children being sexually abused, either by:

a. Incest or

b. Being pushed out to enjoy sex with friends; whether by having boy friends, girl friends, or being used to make money.

6. Children being pushed too soon/too much to become independent at too young an age.

7. Juvenile delinquency.

C. General Problems of Children

1. Dropping out of school

2. Alcohol and drug use

3. Pre-marital relationship and sexually transmitted diseases

4. Rape, homicide, and theft

5. Lack of respect for teachers, elders, and senior citizens

IV. ISLAMIC CONCEPTS

Islam has laid down general concepts and rules to be followed, so that people will live in peace and harmony. Islam has also laid down specific injunctions that need to be followed. As for the family, the following are some of the major concepts:

A. The family is the cornerstone and the foundation of a social, cultural and religious structure in the society.

B. God created man from a single soul and made the spouse a mate for him.

C. Then God created from the same soul, men and women in large numbers. Therefore, we should fear, respect, and appreciate Allah for His creation.

D. From among His signs are mates (spouses), who have been created, so that they may dwell in tranquility. To fulfill this objective, He has made compassion, love, sympathy, concern and mercy between the two spouses.

E. Allah has made all of the above so that we may think, ponder, contemplate and reflect.

F. There is to be no sexual relationship before marriage, just as there is no extra-marital relationship (after marriage).

G. The Married Life In Islam is a matter of worship, just like praying, fasting and other religious acts. Hence, it

11

is considered to be the fulfillment of the faith of the individuals.

H. Marriage is not only for the newly-wed couples, but their extended families have to be included. This means that the relatives of each become blood relatives to both.

I. Love between the couple starts after marriage. If love starts before marriage, it will definitely stop after marriage.

J. During the process of courtship (khitbah), and before performing the marriage ceremony (Nikah), the two individuals are to know one another. However, there should be no privacy between them. The members of the two families are to be included also.

K. For an official marriage to take place, an officiation has to be performed, and there should be witnesses, preferably from their blood relatives.

L. The concept of "mahr" or dowry is to be offered by the groom to the bride. It is a token commitment of the groom to the bride that he is to be responsible for the family.

M. For marriage, one should look for the girl who is compassionate, pious, tender and bashful.

N. After the marriage ceremony takes place, or after the marriage has been consummated, it is recommended that a "Walimah" is to be offered. It is a dinner where relatives and friends are invited.

O. It is recommended that Khitbah (courtship) and Nikah (marriage) ceremonies and the Walimah be publicized. The marriage is not just a union of the two.

P. Marriage is for worldly and Heavenly benefits, both at the same time.

Q. Marriage helps a person to live a stable life; morally, socially, culturally, spiritually, economically, and biologically, etc.

V. PREVENTATIVE MEASURES

In order to have solid and stable families, certain preventative measures have to be taken into consideration: some of these measures are the following:

A. The sources and causes that may lead a person to sex involvement are to be nullified from the society, such as: pornography, adult books, X-rated programs, Playboy and Penthouse type magazines, mixed swimming, mixed dancing, mixed sports activities, alcohol, drugs and the like.

B. The helping (by parents and friends) of young men and women to get married and to have a stable life.

C. Helping young people to have the necessities of life, such as jobs, housing, transportation, education, medical subsidies, etc.

D. Enforcing the laws strictly on everyone.

VI. CHOOSING THE RIGHT SPOUSE

When a person is seeking marriage, he should look for the pious girl; otherwise, he will be in trouble for most of his life. Our beloved Prophet (pbuh) informed us that people may seek girls for marriage for one of the following categories:

A. beauty;

B. position and status in the society;

C. wealth and property; or,

D. piety and righteousness.

Our beloved Prophet informed us that whoever is to be blessed, to enjoy life and to live in peace and harmony, is to seek the pious girl. It is easy to convince her with the teachings of Islam.

As far as beauty is concerned, it is a relative matter, i.e., what might appear beautiful to one person, may appear to be ugly to another. Beauty vanishes with time. After marriage, the physical beauty diminishes and the two spouses should be looking for the beauty of the heart, mind and spirit. People do look for peace of mind through mutual understanding. This happy life can't be achieved except through piety and righteousness.

As far as her position in society is concerned, one may marry a daughter of a president, a member of parliament, a congressman, a senator, a governor, a mayor, with the hope of getting fame, position, and a reputation. Or, one may get married to an American girl for her being American to get the Green Card of America. All these approaches are not recommended in Islam. Whoever is now in a good position, may not be so later, and one has to look for happiness and felicity for the rest of his/her life.

As far as wealth and property are concerned, they will not bring happiness and peace of mind. A person would be busy in managing them, and he would be continually worried about them. Wealth and property are not eternal. A person who is wealthy today, can be poor tomorrow. Moreover, wealth and property are a matter of relativity to different people.

Hence, to look for the righteous and pious girl would be the answer for peace, happiness and felicity. In this respect, the Prophet (pbuh) said:

> *"A woman is to be married for one of the four categories: for her wealth, for her reputation, for her beauty, or for her piety. Win the one with piety, so as to be blessed."*
>
> *(Reported by Bukhari and Muslim)*

VII. WHY TO DEVELOP A FAMILY

The reasons for a person to develop a family are many, among which are the following:

15

A. It is the natural way that Allah has instituted instinctively within the human race. In this regard, Allah says in Surah Al-Nisa' (Women):

بِسْمِ اللّٰهِ النَّاسُ اتَّقُوا رَبَّكُمُ الَّذِي خَلَقَكُم مِّن نَّفْسٍ وَاحِدَةٍ وَخَلَقَ مِنْهَا
زَوْجَهَا وَبَثَّ مِنْهُمَا رِجَالًا كَثِيرًا وَنِسَاءً وَاتَّقُوا اللّٰهَ الَّذِي تَسَاءَلُونَ
بِهِ وَالْأَرْحَامَ إِنَّ اللّٰهَ كَانَ عَلَيْكُمْ رَقِيبًا ﴿١﴾

O mankind! reverence your Guardian Lord, Who created you from a single person, created, of like nature, his mate, and from them scattered (like seeds) countless men and women; reverence God, through Whom you demand your mutual (rights), and (reverence) the wombs (that bore you): for God ever watches over you.

(4:1)

B. The natural way that Prophet Muhammad (pbuh) recommended was his tradition (Sunnah). He said:

Marriage is part of my tradition; whoever refrains from my tradition, he is not part of me.

C. Prophet Muhammad (pbuh) encouraged young people to get married, saying:

O young people! whosoever can afford (marriage) should get married, as it helps casting down one's own gaze, and it protects one's own sex organs; and whosoever can not

16

afford marriage, has to fast as it is a protection for him.

D. To get married and to have children is an inherent feeling of survival on this planet. It helps to bring-up the children to inherit this planet and to transfer the knowledge to the children. For Muslim parents, they want children to pray for them, to make Du'a' (supplication) and to duplicate their efforts and knowledge. In so doing, parents will be rewarded by Allah. Good children can be a protection for their parents on the Day of Judgement, too. Prophet Muhammad (pbuh) said:

> *When a child of Adam dies, his deeds are over except for three: perpetual charity, useful knowledge, or a good child who makes Du'a' for him.*

Children are being admonished to pray for the sake of their parents. Allah says in the Qur'an in Surah Ibrahim the following:

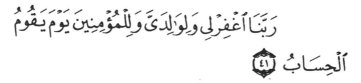

Our Lord! Forgive me and my parents and believers on the day when the account is cast.

(14:41)

When Muslims die, they want their children to continue making Du'a' for them. This will be one of the ways to get the blessings of Allah.

17

VIII. HUSBAND-WIFE RELATIONS

The relation of the two spouses in Islam is that of:

A) Compassion(**widd**);

B) Mercy (**Rahmah**);

C) Leadership with the responsibility imposed upon the husband (**Qiwamah**); and,

D) Consultation (**shura**).

The first two characteristics are explained in the Qur'an in Surah Al-Rūm (Romans):

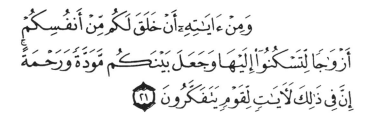

And among His signs is this, that He created for you mates from among yourselves, that you may dwell in tranquility with them, and He has put love and mercy between your (hearts): Truly in that are signs for those who reflect.

(30:21)

As far as leadership is concerned, Allah has made it

18

clear. This type of leadership is nothing more than the responsibility that the husband should assume. In this respect, Allah says in the Surah Al-Nisa' (The Women), the following:

الرِّجَالُ قَوَّمُونَ عَلَى النِّسَاءِ بِمَا فَضَّلَ اللهُ بَعْضَهُمْ عَلَى بَعْضٍ وَبِمَا أَنفَقُوا مِنْ أَمْوَالِهِمْ ...

Men are the protectors and maintainers of women, because God has given the one more (strength) than the other, and because they support them from their means... **(4:34)**

As far as the Shura (consultation) is concerned, Allah has demanded that without Shura, there will not be a happy house and a happy family. He said in the Qur'an, in Surah Al-Shura (Consultation), the following:

وَالَّذِينَ اسْتَجَابُوا لِرَبِّهِمْ وَأَقَامُوا الصَّلَوٰةَ وَأَمْرُهُمْ شُورَىٰ بَيْنَهُمْ وَمِمَّا رَزَقْنَاهُمْ يُنفِقُونَ ﴿٣٨﴾

And who conduct their affairs by mutual consultation.

(42:38)

IX. PARENT-CHILD RELATIONSHIP

In order to have a good relationship between parents and children, one has to build up a bridge of training, discipline,

19

love, sympathy, concern, affection and mutual understanding. The following is a summary of the teachings of Islam which deal with this subject:

A. Training and upbringing of children according to the teachings of Islam. Prophet Muhammad (pbuh) said:

> *Order your children to pray while they are seven years old, punish them if they negate prayer when they are ten years old, and separate them in their sleeping places.*

B. Children should be raised properly according to the teachings of Islam so that they will be a source of protection for their parents. In this regard, Allah says in Surah Al-Tahreem (Prohibition), the following:

يَٰٓأَيُّهَا ٱلَّذِينَ ءَامَنُوا۟ قُوٓا۟ أَنفُسَكُمْ وَأَهْلِيكُمْ
نَارًا وَقُودُهَا ٱلنَّاسُ وَٱلْحِجَارَةُ عَلَيْهَا مَلَٰٓئِكَةٌ غِلَاظٌ شِدَادٌ
لَّا يَعْصُونَ ٱللَّهَ مَآ أَمَرَهُمْ وَيَفْعَلُونَ مَا يُؤْمَرُونَ ٦

> *O you who believe! Save yourselves and your families from a Fire whose fuel is men and stones, over which are (appointed) Angels stern and severe, who flinch not (from executing) the commands they receive from God, but do (precisely) what they are commanded.* (66:6)

20

C. Children are to respect and honor their parents at all times, whether they are alive or dead, or whether they are young, old or senile. In Islam, there is no problem of generation gap. Muslims are to live in peace and harmony within their families.

   1. The teachings of Islam demand from the Muslims to honor their parents and to be kind to them. Allah says in Surah Al-Isra':

وَقَضَىٰ رَبُّكَ أَلَّا تَعْبُدُوٓاْ إِلَّآ إِيَّاهُ وَبِٱلْوَٰلِدَيْنِ إِحْسَٰنًاۚ إِمَّا يَبْلُغَنَّ عِندَكَ ٱلْكِبَرَ أَحَدُهُمَآ أَوْ كِلَاهُمَا فَلَا تَقُل لَّهُمَآ أُفٍّ وَلَا تَنْهَرْهُمَا وَقُل لَّهُمَا قَوْلًا كَرِيمًا ۝

Your Lord has decreed that you worship none but Him, and that you be kind to parents. Whether one or both of them attain old age in your life, say not to them a word of contempt, nor repel them, but address them in terms of honor.

(17:23)

   2. Islam teaches that parents are to advise their children to be obedient to God, good to their parents in all types of situations, good to people, humble, and to live an honest and sincere life. In this respect, Allah has given us a good example of Luqman, the wise person and how he advised his

21

his son. Allah says in Surah Luqman:

وَإِذْ قَالَ
لُقْمَنُ لِابْنِهِ وَهُوَ يَعِظُهُ يَبُنَيَّ لَا تُشْرِكْ بِاللَّهِ إِنَّ الشِّرْكَ
لَظُلْمٌ عَظِيمٌ ﴿١٣﴾

*Behold, Luqman said to his son by way of advice:
'O my son! Join not in worship (others) with
God; for false worship is indeed the highest
wrong-doing.* (31:13)

You may read this story from Ayah 13 through 19, in
the same Surah (Surah Luqman).

In treating parents with due respect, I do invite you to
read the story of the three friends who went for a picnic and
were trapped in a cave. I want you to read the story of a
man who came to the Prophet complaining about his father's
loan. Also read the story of the person carrying one of his
parents on his shoulder while making Tawaf around the
Ka'abah.

These three stories are indeed worth reading and
applying their meaning in one's private life.

X. A PEACEFUL FAMILY

In order to have a peaceful family life, one has to
recognize that a person is affected by several factors. Some
of these are the following:

A. Genetics and heredity before and after marriage;

B. Food and Diets;

C. Environment and society; and,

D. Hidayah or guidance from Allah for those who deserve it.

XI. <u>FINAL REMARKS</u>

Islam has encouraged Muslims to marry, to have children, and to raise them in an honest life. Marriage is sacred and it is an act of worship. If its rules and regulations are followed with good intention, a person will be rewarded. A happy life will be established between the new couples and a better family life will prevail between the parents and their children.

That this is indeed a Qur'an most honorable.
In a Book well-guarded...
[Qur'an. 56:77-78]

Chapter 2
KHUTBATUN NIKAH

*And it is He Who has power
over all things.* [Qur'an, 5:120]

I. INTRODUCTION

The meaning of the word Khutbatun Nikah is a sermon (speech) to be given just before marriage vows are to take place. The Imam (Ma'zoon), acting as an official person to perform the marriage vows for the young couple, is to give a religious sermon to the people attending the marriage officiation. This is a Sunnah (Tradition) of the Prophet (pbuh).

The Imam is to recite to the audience a few verses from the Qur'an and a few from Ahadith. He is to remind them of their obligation to each other as husband and wife. He is to encourage the young adults to get married as soon as possible.

After reading the vows, he is to pray for their happiness. He then sign the official papers with the presence of the guardian (wakeel), two witnesses, and his signature.

It is recommended that a pre-marriage agreement is to be signed and notorized. The dowery (Mahr) is to be agreed upon, and to be recorded in the state as well as in the masjid.

II. QUR'AN ON MARRIAGE

Allah says in the Qur'an in Surah Al-Nisa' (Women) the following:

25

بِسْمِ اللّٰهِ يَتَأَيُّهَا النَّاسُ اتَّقُوا رَبَّكُمُ الَّذِي خَلَقَكُم مِّن نَّفْسٍ وَاحِدَةٍ وَخَلَقَ مِنْهَا
زَوْجَهَا وَبَثَّ مِنْهُمَا رِجَالًا كَثِيرًا وَنِسَاءً وَاتَّقُوا اللّٰهَ الَّذِي تَسَاءَلُونَ
بِهِ وَالْأَرْحَامَ إِنَّ اللّٰهَ كَانَ عَلَيْكُمْ رَقِيبًا ۞

O mankind! Reverence your Guardian Lord, who created you from a single person, created, of like nature, his mate, and from them twain scattered (like seeds) countless men and women; reverence God, through Whom you demand your mutual (rights), and (reverence) the wombs (that bore you): for God ever watches over you. **(4:1)**

Allah also says in the Qur'an in Surah Al-Rum (The Romans):

وَمِنْ ءَايَاتِهِ أَنْ خَلَقَ لَكُم مِّنْ أَنفُسِكُمْ
أَزْوَاجًا لِّتَسْكُنُوا إِلَيْهَا وَجَعَلَ بَيْنَكُم مَّوَدَّةً وَرَحْمَةً
إِنَّ فِي ذَلِكَ لَآيَاتٍ لِّقَوْمٍ يَتَفَكَّرُونَ ۞

And among His signs is this, that He created for you mates from among yourselves, that you may dwell in tranquillity with them, and He has put love and mercy between your (hearts): Verily in that are signs for those who reflect.

(30:21)

26

In these two Ayat Allah is reminding people of the following:

A. He created us all from a single soul.

B. He created the spouse mate from the same soul.

C. He created from the same soul men and women in large number.

D. We should fear, respect and appreciate Allah and His creation.

E. From among His signs, spouse mates were created so that they may dwell in tranquility.

F. He made compassion, love, sympathy, concern and mercy between the two spouses.

G. He made all the above so that we may think, ponder, contemplate and reflect.

III. BENEFITS OF MARRIAGE

As far as marriage is concerned, Islam encourages people to get married as soon as possible. Some of the major benefits that one gets through marriage are the following:

A. One may complete his faith by getting married according to the Hadith of Prophet Muhammad (pbuh):

Whoever Allah bestows upon with a good woman, he is helped by Allah to fulfill half of his religion; hence, he should fear Allah in the second half of his religion.

B. It is part of the Sunnah of the Prophet (pbuh). This means that when a person gets married he will be rewarded more. The Prophet (pbuh) said:

Whoever likes my way is to follow it, and one of my way is to get married.

C. Marriage is part of worship, and whoever gets married will be rewarded by performing his duties within the matrimonial life.

Narrated by Abi Zarr Al-Ghaffari (May Allah be pleased with him) that the Prophet (pbuh) said: '...even you will be rewarded for your sexual relation (with your wife).' They (followers) asked, 'O Messenger of Allah, if any one of us get sexual satisfaction he would be rewarded?' He said: 'If he uses it in unlawful ways, would he not be punished? Therefore, if he uses it in lawful ways, he would be rewarded.' Reported by Muslim

D. Through marriage a person will protect himself, control his lust and cast down his sight. He will be able to control and to direct his sexual urges in the right direction. He will protect himself from getting involved in Haram against himself or against others. In this regard, Prophet Muhammad (pbuh) said:

28

Narrated by Abdullah bin 'Umar saying: We were with the Prophet (pbuh) as young people without the necessities of the worldly affairs. The Messenger of Allah said to us: 'O young people! Whoever is able to assume responsibility, let him marry. Marriage helps protect the sight, and sex organs. Whoever can not, let him fast. Fasting is a means of protection.'

IV. OTHER MATTERS

In Islam the groom is to offer a dowry (mahr) to the bride to assume his responsibility and his leadership of the family. The mahr should be minimum. It was reported that the Prophet (pbuh) commanded the grooms to offer mahr to the brides as little as an iron ring. This sunnah of the Prophet (pbuh), when it is followed, will bring happiness to the newly developed family. The Qur'an states that "mahr" is to be given by the groom to the bride. In this regard, Allah says the following in Surah Al-Nisa' (The Women):

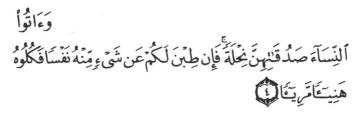

And give the women on marriage their dower as a free gift; but if they, of their own good pleasure, remit any part of it to you, take it and enjoy it with right good cheer.   *(4:4)*

The following hadith is very clear about the making of happiness for marrying a girl.

> *Narrated by Aiysha (May Allah be pleased with her) that the Prophet (pbuh) said: Blessings of a woman are: the mahr is minimum, the marriage performance is easy, and her manners are good; while the unfortunate marriage from a woman is to have: expensive mahr, difficulty in marriage performance, and her bad manners.*

Muslims are encouraged to have children within the marriage. The concept of birth control is not accepted in Islam. However, family planning is allowed and permitted. When we are planning to have children, one has to remember that the parents have to raise them according to the teachings of Islam. We have to remember here the Hadith of Prophet Muhammad whereby he encouraged Muslims to increase the number of their Muslim children so that he will be proud of all during the Day of Judgement. He said:

> *The Prophet (pbuh) said: Get married to the compassionate and the potent, as I will be proud of you in front of the other nations in the Day of Judgement.*

V. FINAL REMARKS

I do encourage everyone to read more of the Qur'an and of the Hadith. I do encourage everyone to study the Sirah of the Prophet in his private life as well as in his public life, so as to imitate him, emulate him, respect him, and be rewarded by Allah. I pray to Allah to accept this marriage that we are performing. I pray to Allah to help the couple to live in peace and harmony under the Shari'ah of Islam.

I pray to Allah to bless and reward all of you who are observing the Nikah ceremony.

After the Nikah performance make a Du'a for the newly wed couple.

Narrated by Abu Hurairah (May Allah be pleased with him) that the Prophet (pbuh) used to say when a person gets married: "May Allah bless for you what you got; May Allah bless you, May Allah unite you both on the good.

"...And help one another in furthering virtue
and God consciousness, and do not help one
another in furthering evil and enmity..."
[Qur'an, 5:2]

31

Chapter 3
CONTRACEPTION

And it is He Who has power
over all things. **[Qur'an, 5:120]**

I. GENERAL

The subject of contraception may be very sensitive todiscuss from a religious aspect without going into the medical aspects. One must discuss the different methods used in contraception, and the side effects that may occur. Then one must determine whether each method and procedure is acceptable from the religious point of view or not.

Islam is a total and a complete way of life. It is a comprehensive system and code of ethics and morality. A determination of the Halal (lawful) or Haram (unlawful) nature of something must rely on the Qur'an, Hadith, and Sunnah of the Prophet. If the information is not found in any of them, then one must use analogy (Qiyas). One should also study the decisions the Muslim 'Ulama' in different parts of the world.

In this chapter, the two authors are presenting the medical and the religious aspects concerning the different varieties of contraceptives. The medical discussions has been kept brief. For more information, the reader is requested t consult his/her physician. For each type of contraceptive analysed, the term "Failure rate" refers to the number of pregnancies that would occur per 100 couples using that method in one year.

We pray to Allah (s.w.t.) to accept our humble efforts and forgive us for our shortcomings.

We start with the medical definition of "contraception" as defined in the Encyclopedia of Medicine, published by the

Medical Association, 1989 edition.

"[Contraception is] the control of fertility to prevent pregnancy. There are various contraceptive menthods that work in different ways, but their basic action is either to stop the sperm and the ovum from meeting in the fallopian tube (thus preventing conception or fertilization) or to prevent a fertilized ovum from implanting in the lining of the uterrus."

II. ISLAMIC VIEWS ON CONTRACEPTION

The term "Family Planning" refers to contraception used by a husband and wife to plan a family by spacing pregnancies. The term "birth control", on the other hand connotates the use of contraception to avoid pregancy as a result of sexual relations, and may take the place outside the marriage. Islamically, any attempt to use contraception as a means of promoting promiscuity is unacceptable. According to Islam, the natural feelings between a man and a woman are to be channeled into the institution of marriage. A husband and wife may find enjoyment in each other, but marital relations must be to procreate. Any children resulting from marital relations should be accepted as gifts from Allah (swt) and should be brought into this world as new Muslims. Islam may allow some "family planning" to make it more feasible, economically, socially, and maritally, to raise a family successful according to the principles of Islam. However, we must study each method before giving an opinion.

III. CONTRACEPTIVE METHODS

The various contraceptive methods available today are listed below. To facilitate discussion these methods will be catagorized by those which prevent conception and those which work after conception has already taken place.

A. Preventive Methods
The contraceptive methods that prevent fertilization of the ovum are:

1. Abstinence
2. Rhythm methods or Natural Family Planning
3. Withdrawal
4. Spermicides
5. Male and Female Condom
6. Sponge
7. Diaphragm
8. Cervical Cap
9. The Pill
10. Depo Provera Shot
11. Norplant
12. Tubal Sterilization
13. Vasectomy

B. Post Conception Methods
The conceptive methods that work after the ovum has been fertilized are:

14. Intra-uterine contraceptive devices (IUD), i.e Lippes' Loop, Safe T Coil, CU 7, and Progestasert.
15. RU 486

16. Abortion

The various methods of contraceptive used today are discussed below, first medically, then Islamically. All forms of contraception must be used with the agreement of both the husband and wife.

1. Abstinence: Abstinence means avoiding marital relations for a period of time. This method is the best and the safest method. Obviously this is not desirable for husband or wife except for short term.

2. Naural Family Planning: This is a way of telling on which days of the month a woman is most likely to get pregnant and avoid having sex on those days. The method involves a woman checking her body temperature on a daily basis and also checking on the quality of cervical mucus. The failure rate is approximately 15%. This is one of the methods with the least side effects and does not require a physician's assistance after the initial consultation.

Religiously speaking it is acceptable.

3. Withdrawal: This method was practiced by the early Muslims to avoid pregnancy. This method was reported to the Prophet, and he did not object to it. It is a safe method and has no negative side effects. The failure rate is 15%.

4. Spermicides: Spermicides are available in foam, cream , jelly, or tablet form to be inserted into the vagina. Spermicides kill the sperm before fertilization. The failure rate is approximately 15%.

5. **Male and Female condoms**: Condoms are latex convering for either the male or female genetalia for use during marital relations. The failure rate is approximately 15%. The use of condoms in combination with other methods of contraception greatly lessens the failure rate and prevents the sexual transmission of disease.

6. Sponge: A small, round specially made sponge already filled with spermicide. It is placed in the vagina over the cervix. Failure rate is approximately 15%. It is considered as one of the preventative methods used to prevent fertilization. In this process the sperms are killed before reaching the ovum.

7. Diaphragm: A diaphragm is a round rubber cup that is placed in the vagina. The diaphragm are availalbe in different sizes and the appropriate size must be measured and prescribed by the physician or a trained nurse. The woman must be taught how to use it. The diaphragm keeps the sperm away from the cervix and uterus. Failure rate is approximately 10%.

8. Cervical Cap: This is also a rubber cup and works like a diaphragm but it is smaller and fitted onto the woman's cervix. A doctor or a trained nurse must select the right size and teach the woman how to use it. Failure rate is approximately 10%.

9. The Pill: The pill prevents the release of eggs from the woman's ovaries. It provides 24 hours per day protection. It must be taken everyday, preferbly the same time every day. The failure rate is approximately 1%-2%. There are many varieties of pills on the market. The word pill means a group of oral drug preparations containing a progesterone often combined with an estrogen which is taken by the woman. All types of oral contraceptives, combined pills and minipills are commonly known as the "pill."

The combined pill increases the level of estrogen and progesterone in the body. Therefore it interferes with the production by the pituitary gland of two gonadotropin hormones called follicle stimulating hormone (FSH) and luteinizing hormone (LH). This action in turn prevents ovulation.

The pill also makes menstrual cycles more regular. It may lessen bleeding and painful cramps, and is often prescribed for non-contraceptive use for these advantages. The Pill is also know to prevent development of varian cysts. A few women who take estrogen containing pills may experience nausea and vomiting, weight gain, depression, breast swelling, reduced sex drive, increased appetite, cramps in th legs and abdomen, headaches, and dizziness. More serious but rare adverse effects of these pills is the risk of a thrombosis causing a stroke, embolism, or myocardinal infarction (heart attack), heart disease or cause hypertension, gallstones, jaundice, and extremely rarely, liver tumor.

Adverse effects are more likely to occur with high doses of estrogen, low estrogen preparations are prescribed whenever possible. Women taking oral contraceptives should receive regular checkups, including blood pressure, weight check and cervical smear tests.

10. Depo Provera: Depo Provera is a medication which is given in the doctor's office by injecting. It provides protection from pregnancy for three months. It works by preventing the release of eggs from the ovary and changing the quality of the cervical mucus. The failure rate is approximately 1%.

11. Norplant: Norplant is a set of six small plastic tubes loaded with medication. These capsules are implanted under the skin of the woman's upper arm under local anesthesia. It provides 24 hours per day protection for five years. Failure rate is less than 1%. This type of medicinal approach does necessitate the use of a hormone called progestogen (i.e. progesterone). They make the cervical mucus impermeable to sperm and reducing the production of gonadotropin hormones. Accordingly it prevents eggs from ripening in the ovary.

The above mentioned methods number 1 through 11, are all termporary. They may be used to space pregnancies and when the method is discontinued, the woman can get pregant again. Since the Prophet did not object to the withdrawal mehtod, it is inferred that temporay methods of contraception used to space pregnancies are acceptable in Islam. However, there are certain conditions discussed in the final remarks, which must be met. Medically speaking though, all the above mentioned methods have acceptable levels of side effects to warrant the advantages.

12. Tubal Sterilization: The tubal ligation is an operation done for the woman to prevent pregnancy. It can be done immediately after the birth of a baby while the woman is still in the hospital. It can also be done at other times on an outpatient basis. Also known as "having your tubes tied," this procedure blocks the tubes and prevents the egg and the sperm from getting together. Tubal sterilization is permanent. Failure rate is approximately 0-1%.

13. Vasectomy: A vasectomy is a minor surgery done on outpatient basis on the man. The tube connecting the testicles and the penis (vase) is cut. It prevents the release of the sperm. A vasetomy is permanent. It usually starts working within four months after the surgery. Failure rate is approximately 0-1%. This operation may cause psychological problems that affect sexual performance.

The last two methods tubal sterilization and vesectomy are permanent. Any method that leads to permanency is not acceptable to the Islamic Shari'ah unless another pregnancy would create serious danger to the life of the wife. Advanced miscrosurgical reversal and assisted production techniques have made it possible for people to have children after these procedures. Nevertheless, since the intention with these methods is permanent sterilization, they are not acceptable in Islam. For those who don't wish to have more children, have to think twice before considering these procedures. Therefore, it is better to have a termporary arrangement rather than a permanent one. The capacity to have children is a lifetime blessing from Allah and we must not shun away from it for convenience.

14. **IUD**: (Intrauterine Device) An IUD is a piece of plastic manufactured in different shapes (for example Lippes' Loop, Delkon Shield, Progestasert, Safe-T Coil). It is placed in the uterus by the physician or a specially trained nurse. It provides protection 24 hours per day, as long as the IUD is in place. Some of the IUD's are plain plastic such as Lippes' Loop. The others carry copper for additional

protection for example CU 7 and yet others carry hormones such as Progestasert. Most IUDs make the lining of the uterus unsuitable for implantaion of fertilized ovum. Horomone loaded IUDs also prevent ovulation. The failure rate is approximately 2-4%. Immediately after the insertion of IUD there may be heavy bleeding or pain. Menstruation may become irregular, heavier, and more painful. Pelvic inflammatory disease may develope and if not treated promptly may lead to permanent infertility. Many pharmaceutical companies have discontinued the manufacture and sale of IUDs in U.S.A. because of the large number of lawsuits claiming that IUDs have caused serious complications.

15. RU 486: RU 486 is a relatively new medication. It is taken by mouth after the suspected fertilization. It essentially causes a spontaneous miscarriage of an early pregnancy, thus it is also commonly known as the "abortion pill."

16. Post Coital Contraception: This method also known as the "morning after pill" involves high doses of estrogen and progesterone combinations. The hormones are used to upset the fertilization process and to get rid of the possibly already fertilized ovum. It should not be taken without the supervision of a physician. This method of contraceptive is used after matrimonial relations in case of failure or absence of the other contraceptive methods.

The contraceptive methods of IUD, RU 486 and Post-Coital contraception are not acceptable in Islam. These methods are unlawful (Haram) on the basis that they interfere with the developement of a pregnancy after the

41

ovum has been fertilized. Killing the fetus and aborting it is totally Haram.

IV. FINAL REMARKS

Islam advocates the establishment of a solid and a stable family life. Islam also advocates the upbringing of children who will inherit the message of Allah and establish the rules and regulations of Allah on this planet Earth. However, the use of Family Planning may or may not be acceptable in Islam. It depends upon the method used, the medicine being used, and the intension behind using such a method.

When choosing any method of contraception, one must always consider the moral aspect of it. Morality in Islam is a top priority and there can be no compromise. If the method brings harm to the wife or husband, it should not be used at all, whatsoever the method is. If the method of contraception being used caused permanent sterilization for either husband or wife, Islam does not allow it; we must preserve our God-given capacity to procreate - none of us know our future circumstances. Harm also must not come to the conceived fetus. To abort after fertilization is totally unlawful even if it is within the family, and even in the case of incest or rape. The rapist is to be condemned and penalized publicly so as to deter any person in the future from such a barbaric act.

If the intention is fear of becoming poor, Allah assured provision of wealth through the coming of the new child. (Qur'an 17:31). Even if the intention is fear of being already poor, Allah assured the family better provisions will come

42

from heaven for the coming of a new child (Qur'an 6:151)

Finally, it is recommended that before choosing any method a couple should consult a Muslim physicians who is practicing the teachings of Islam and who has Taqwa. The couple also should consult a knowledgeable 'Alim who is well versed in Islamic Shari'ah as well as with the modern science and technology. After consulting all these people, the couple should pray a special salat to Allah requesting guidance. They pray either Salat Haajah or Salat Istikharah (requesting the best of the different methods). Allah will never leave the couple without guidance.

Which none shall touch (The Qur'an) but
those who are clean. [Qur'an, 56:79]

Chapter 4
PARENTS-CHILDREN RELATIONSHIP

I. INTRODUCTION

Parents-children relationship is an association built on cause and effect. It is established on mutual love, affection, sympathy, concern and mercy. It is based on mutual responsibility, duties and obligations. If and when parents assume their responsibilities towards themselves and towards their children, then the children would be raised with honor and dignity. They will feel the love and mercy of their parents. In turn, they will honor their parents and give them respect, esteem and reverence.

A child is a child to his parents no matter how young or old the child is. Parents look at their son as a son no matter how old the son is. The same thing applies to their daughter. On the other hand, a son thinks he is already a grown-up after the age of 16-18. He wants to be independent, and he wants to make decisions by himself without receiving instructions or advice. The same thing applies to a daughter.

Problems might be created between parents and children. Those problems have a cause, but they can be treated and resolved if both parties are willing to listen and to assume their responsibilities towards one another. Sometimes problems are too big to be resolved, but there is nothing impossible in this world.

In this chapter, a series of duties and responsibilities of the parents towards their children are discussed.

We pray to Allah (swt) to bless and reward all of us, and to forgive us for our shortcomings. Ameen.

II. PARENTS DUTIES DURING PREGNANCY

The husband and wife relationship should be at its best. Anything that goes on between them does affect the life of the fetus. Eating habits, type of foods, liquids, smoking and drugs do affect the biological life of the fetus.

No parent should think of abortion when fertilization takes place. Both husband and wife should be grateful to Allah for such a thing that took place. If they are poor, Allah will enrich them. In Surah Al-An'am (The Cattles), Allah (swt) says the following:

$$ وَلَا تَقْتُلُوٓاْ أَوْلَٰدَكُم مِّنْ إِمْلَٰقٍ نَّحْنُ نَرْزُقُكُمْ وَإِيَّاهُمْ $$

...kill not your children on a plea of want: We provide sustenance for you and for them ....

(6:151)

of they are afraid of poverty by having a child they should realize that Allah (swt) will provide them and enrich them in the near future. The Qur'an stipulates the following in Surah Al-Israa'. (Night-Journey)

$$ وَلَا تَقْتُلُوٓاْ أَوْلَٰدَكُمْ خَشْيَةَ إِمْلَٰقٍ نَّحْنُ نَرْزُقُهُمْ وَإِيَّاكُمْ إِنَّ قَتْلَهُمْ كَانَ خِطْـًٔا كَبِيرًا ۝ $$

46

kill not your children for fear of want: We shall provide sustenance for them as well as for you. Verily, the killing of them is a great sin.

(17:31)

For those who abort, they are criminals in the Book of Allah (swt). They are losers. In Surah Al-An'am (The Cattle) Allah says the following:

قَدْ خَسِرَ ٱلَّذِينَ قَتَلُوٓا۟ أَوْلَٰدَهُمْ

سَفَهًۢا بِغَيْرِ عِلْمٍ وَحَرَّمُوا۟ مَا رَزَقَهُمُ ٱللَّهُ ٱفْتِرَآءً عَلَى ٱللَّهِ

قَدْ ضَلُّوا۟ وَمَا كَانُوا۟ مُهْتَدِينَ ۝

Lost are those who slay their children, from folly, without knowledge, and forbid food which Allah has provided for them, inventing (lies) against Allah. They have indeed gone astray and heeded no guidance.

(6:140)

III. DUTIES DURING INFANCY

Parents have duties and responsibilities towards their newly born babies. Some of the major obligations are the following:

A.   The moment a baby is born, the father is to recite Azan in the right ear of the infant. He is also to recite Iqama in the left ear.

B.   Both parents have to select a name which reflects

47

beauty, obedience and praise to Allah.

C. Boys are to be circumcised as soon as possible.

D. A special reception (Aqeeqa) is to be offered to relatives and friends. Such a dinner is offered in praise to Allah for His blessings upon them.

E. The hair of the child is to be shaved and donate money to needy people.

F. The infant is to be nursed by his mother. She should never refuse to do so. Her milk has better nutritional values. Her love for her baby (by hugging and embracing him to her bosom) does reflect attachment to each other. Allah (swt) demanded mothers to nurse their babies for a maximum of two years for those who want to do so. In Sarah Al-Baqarah (The Cow) Allah (swt) says the following:

﷽ وَٱلْوَٰلِدَٰتُ يُرْضِعْنَ أَوْلَٰدَهُنَّ
حَوْلَيْنِ كَامِلَيْنِ لِمَنْ أَرَادَ أَن يُتِمَّ ٱلرَّضَاعَةَ وَعَلَى ٱلْمَوْلُودِ لَهُ رِزْقُهُنَّ
وَكِسْوَتُهُنَّ بِٱلْمَعْرُوفِ لَا تُكَلَّفُ نَفْسٌ إِلَّا وُسْعَهَا لَا تُضَآرَّ
وَٰلِدَةٌ بِوَلَدِهَا وَلَا مَوْلُودٌ لَّهُ بِوَلَدِهِ وَعَلَى ٱلْوَارِثِ مِثْلُ ذَٰلِكَ
فَإِنْ أَرَادَا فِصَالًا عَن تَرَاضٍ مِّنْهُمَا وَتَشَاوُرٍ فَلَا جُنَاحَ عَلَيْهِمَا وَإِنْ
أَرَدتُّمْ أَن تَسْتَرْضِعُوا أَوْلَٰدَكُمْ فَلَا جُنَاحَ عَلَيْكُمْ إِذَا سَلَّمْتُم مَّآ
ءَاتَيْتُم بِٱلْمَعْرُوفِ وَٱتَّقُوا ٱللَّهَ وَٱعْلَمُوا أَنَّ ٱللَّهَ بِمَا تَعْمَلُونَ بَصِيرٌ ﴿٢٣٣﴾

48

The mothers shall give suck to their offspring for two whole years, if the father desires to complete the term. But he shall bear the cost of their food and clothing on equitable terms. No soul shall have a burden laid on it greater than it can bear. No mother shall be treated unfairly on account of her child, Nor father on account of his child. An heir shall be chargeable in the same way, if they both decide on weaning by mutual consent, and after due consultation, there is no blame on them. If they decide on a foster-mother for their offspring, there is no blame on them, provided they pay on equitable terms. But fear Allah Who sees well what you do.

(2:233)

5. If the mother cannot nurse her baby for any medical reasons, then another woman should extend her help to nurse the baby. Allah (swt) revealed such information in the Qur'an in Surah Al-Talaq (Divorce). Allah says the following:

أَسْكِنُوهُنَّ مِنْ حَيْثُ سَكَنتُم مِّن وُجْدِكُمْ وَلَا تُضَارُّوهُنَّ لِتُضَيِّقُوا عَلَيْهِنَّ وَإِن كُنَّ أُوْلَٰتِ حَمْلٍ فَأَنفِقُوا عَلَيْهِنَّ حَتَّىٰ يَضَعْنَ حَمْلَهُنَّ فَإِنْ أَرْضَعْنَ لَكُمْ فَآتُوهُنَّ أُجُورَهُنَّ وَأْتَمِرُوا بَيْنَكُم بِمَعْرُوفٍ وَإِن تَعَاسَرْتُمْ فَسَتُرْضِعُ لَهُۥٓ أُخْرَىٰ ۝ لِيُنفِقْ ذُو سَعَةٍ مِّن سَعَتِهِۦ وَمَن قُدِرَ عَلَيْهِ رِزْقُهُۥ فَلْيُنفِقْ مِمَّآ ءَاتَىٰهُ ٱللَّهُ لَا يُكَلِّفُ ٱللَّهُ نَفْسًا إِلَّا مَآ ءَاتَىٰهَا سَيَجْعَلُ ٱللَّهُ بَعْدَ عُسْرٍ يُسْرًا ۝

49

Let the women live (in 'iddah) in the same style as you live. According to your means, annoy them not, so as to restrict them. And if they carry (life in their wombs), then spend (your substance) on them until they deliver their burden, and if they suckle your (offspring), give them their recompense and take mutual counsel together according to what is just and reasonable. And if you find yourselves in difficulties, let another woman suckle (the child) on the (father's) behalf.

Let the man of means spend according to his means, and the man whose resources are restricted, let him spend according to what Allah has given him. Allah puts no burden on any person beyond what he has given him. After a difficulty, Allah will soon grant relief.　　　　　　　　　　　　*(65: 6-7)*

H.　　In case another woman has nursed that baby, then the latter is unlawful for him to marry any of his sisters from his nursing mother. If the baby is a girl, she is unlawful to marry any of her brothers from her nursing mother. In Surah Al-Nisa' (The Women) Allah (swt) says the following:

حُرِّمَتْ عَلَيْكُمْ أُمَّهَـٰتُكُمْ
وَبَنَاتُكُمْ وَأَخَوَاتُكُمْ وَعَمَّاتُكُمْ وَخَـٰلَـٰتُكُمْ وَبَنَاتُ
ٱلْأَخِ وَبَنَاتُ ٱلْأُخْتِ وَأُمَّهَـٰتُكُمُ ٱلَّـٰتِىٓ أَرْضَعْنَكُمْ
وَأَخَوَاتُكُم مِّنَ ٱلرَّضَـٰعَةِ وَأُمَّهَـٰتُ نِسَآئِكُمْ

وَرَبَـٰٓئِبُكُمُ ٱلَّـٰتِى فِى حُجُورِكُم مِّن نِّسَآئِكُمُ
ٱلَّـٰتِى دَخَلۡتُم بِهِنَّ فَإِن لَّمۡ تَكُونُواْ دَخَلۡتُم بِهِنَّ
فَلَا جُنَاحَ عَلَيۡكُمۡ وَحَلَـٰٓئِلُ أَبۡنَآئِكُمُ ٱلَّذِينَ
مِنۡ أَصۡلَـٰبِكُمۡ وَأَن تَجۡمَعُواْ بَيۡنَ ٱلۡأُخۡتَيۡنِ
إِلَّا مَا قَدۡ سَلَفَۗ إِنَّ ٱللَّهَ كَانَ غَفُورًا رَّحِيمًا ۩

*Prohibited to you (for marriage) are your mothers,
daughters, sisters, father's sisters, mother's sisters,
brothers, daughters, sister's daughters, and foster-
mothers who gave you suck; foster-sisters, your
wives' mothers, your step-daughters under your
guardianship, born of your wives to whom you have
gone in. No prohibition if you have not gone in.
Those who have been wives of your sons proceeding
from your loin; and two sisters in wedlock at one
and the same time, except for what is past, for Allah
is Oft-Forgiving, Most Merciful.*

(4:23)

IV. DUTIES DURING CHILDHOOD

Children during the ages of 2-7 are in a state of
mimicking. They are smart. They want to learn by touching,
playing, seeing, observing, hearing and doing things without
knowing the danger. They are very innocent.

Parents are to play with them. They are to narrate to
them story after story using the language of a child. Such
stories should have moral aspects of love and respect,
helping the needy, visiting the sick, giving money to the
poor, etc. Parents are to refrain from mentioning any scary

stories. They should teach them love and obedience to Allah as well as the love for the Prophet (pbuh), love for his family and his companions.

Parents are to offer daily prayers while the child is imitating and practicing salat with the parents. Parents are to take the child to the Masjid for Salat and especially that to Jumu'ah Salat. They are to send the child to a full time Muslim school. In such an Islamic atmosphere, the child will develop his attitude, behavior and manners.

Parents are to refrain from any bad language or from arguments among themselves or even with their children. Parents are to introduce their children to other family members, mainly: grandparents, uncles, aunts, cousins, nephews, nieces, etc.

V. DUTIES DURING PRE-ADOLESCENCE

The age of children before reaching adolescence is a sensitive and delicate age. It is the age between 7-14 years old. Their brain, their body, and their hormones are to be developed. Children are very sensitive to their body changes and their mental understanding.

Parents are to be more concerned about their children's development. They are to be close to them. They are to discuss with their children some major topics of decency, morality, dress code, respect to others, cleanliness, boys-girls relationship, and other related matters.

52

Parents are to teach their children the basic teachings of Islam, mainly pillars of Islam, pillars of Imam, and branches of Imam, etc. Children are to pray five times a day individually or preferably collectively with parents. They are to read and memorize certain chapters from the Qur'an.

Children are to be trained to fast the month of Ramadan as much as they can. They are to develop a habit of fasting the month of Ramadan, like others. They should learn the rules and regulations of fastings.. Zakat.. prayers.. and Hajj. Parents should try to take their children at that age to perform Umra and/or Hajj to Makkah.

Brothers and sisters are to behave with respect towards one another. They should have individual rooms for sleeping and studying. They should try to build a sense of responsibility inside the house. They should know how to help in fixing the house. Such activities include: dishwashing, ironing, laundry, vacuuming, cooking, table manners, room preparation and making up bed. Children are to learn how to save money and how to be contented with what they have.

Parents should take their children and show them the homeless people who live on the streets without food and shelter. Then and only then they will be satisfied with whatever they have. At the same time, they should learn how to be generous to the needy and poor. They should be trained to give donations, and contributions to build Masajid and Muslim schools. Sadaqa and charity is to be given to relief organizations in different parts of the world.

The children should go with their parents to visit the sick in hospitals or even in their houses. Also, parents should take their children to cemeteries and explain to them the process of death and life and death. They should not scare them of it. It is a life cycle that all of us are to go through.

Parents should advise their children to study well and be among the best in their academic achievements. They should help them to keep away from kids who are bad. They are to be informed about the harmful effects of drugs, alcohol and smoking. They should refrain completely from getting involved in any of these types of problems.

Parents should take their children to public parks and play with them, as well as camping with other Muslim families. Protection on one side and positive involvement on the other side are the keys of success in this world. With the mercy of Allah, children will be saved from being lost.

VI. DUTIES DURING ADOLESCENCE

The adolescent life of a child is the most difficult stage of the life-cycle of any human being. It could be a rebellious stage and a stage of refusal of any and everything they have learned. It could be a stage of independency and at the same time an age of laziness and total dependency. Some children may want to decide for themselves. They want to try and find out for themselves and by themselves. They may refuse any advice, instructions or orders. At the same time, they want their parents to give them anything and everything they wish to have.

This age is the age of ego and the age of boasting. Many children want everything for themselves. They don't care for others. They may fight with one another as brothers and sisters in the same house.

At the same time, this age is the age of puberty. Girls may already have their menses. Their femininity is already showing on their faces and bodies. Boys masculinity does show on their faces and bodies too. They should learn how to cope with all these biological changes.

Parents are to recognize that their children are grown up. They cannot receive any instructions. Parents should treat their children as brothers and sisters to them. Communication with logic and common sense are the key to success. Parents are no more to give orders, but to discuss and share the discussions with their children.

Parents should be humble to accept the views of their children. They should encourage them to discuss mutual subjects with respect to each one's point of view. Whenever any child says something good, should be complimented and encouraged.

Parents should train their children to be leaders. Leadership starts by giving them the chance to be Imam to the parents and to the whole family. This means that children should be trained how to lead Salat in congregation. They should know how to give Azan, Iqama and lead Salat.

VII. FINAL REMARKS

The information summarized in this chapter are taken from Qur'an, Sunnah, Seerah, and Fiqh. Due to the shortage of space, it was not possible to quote all the Ayat and the Ahadith. Along with the experience as parents, grandparents, and as family counsellors, we were able to shed some lights on these stages of developments of the children.

Parents are the responsible ones for the mistakes of their children. The formers are encouraged to assume their responsibilities as parents before it is to late.

Children are usually the mirror images of their parents. Exceptional cases do exist. Parents cannot expect their children to be good unless they themselves are good. If parents don't pray, they should not expect their children to pray. If husband and wife are fighting, they should expect their children to do so among themselves. At the same time, children will never respect their parents.

All what we hope and pray that each one of us will take the initiative and do the best. The rest is in the hands of Allah (swt).

Allah is the Light of the Heavens and Earth.

Chapter 5
RESPECT OF PARENTS

In the Name of Allah and Praise Be to Allah.

I. INTRODUCTION

In America there are many special days set aside to honor and appreciate special people. Some of these are: Father's Day, Mother's Day, Grandfather's Day, Grandmother's Day, Memorial Day, Labor Day, etc. We do realize the significance of these occasions and we recognize the ideas, ideals, and philosophies of such days. We appreciate the efforts of those who initiated these occasions for the recognition and appreciation of special people.

As for the appreciation of parents, we admire the efforts of children who remember their parents on such occasions by sending them greeting cards and gifts. However, we hope that the appreciation is not for one single day in a year, but for every day throughout the year.

II. PARENTS IN QUR'AN

A Muslim child should respect and appreciate his or her parents every day throughout the year. Allah asked human beings to recognize their parents after recognition Allah Himself. Throughout the Qur'an, we notice that parents are mentioned with appreciation and with respect, even if they are senile. In Surah Al-Isra' (Children of Israel) there is a very beautiful description of how parents are to be treated. Allah (swt) says:

﴿ وَقَضَىٰ رَبُّكَ أَلَّا تَعْبُدُوٓا۟ إِلَّآ إِيَّاهُ وَبِٱلْوَٰلِدَيْنِ إِحْسَٰنًا إِمَّا يَبْلُغَنَّ عِندَكَ ٱلْكِبَرَ أَحَدُهُمَآ أَوْ كِلَاهُمَا فَلَا تَقُل لَّهُمَآ ﴾

أَفٍّ وَلَا تَنْهَرْهُمَا وَقُل لَّهُمَا قَوْلًا كَرِيمًا ۞ وَٱخْفِضْ لَهُمَا جَنَاحَ ٱلذُّلِّ مِنَ ٱلرَّحْمَةِ وَقُل رَّبِّ ٱرْحَمْهُمَا كَمَا رَبَّيَانِي صَغِيرًا ۞

Your Lord had decreed, that you worship none save Him, and (that you show) kindness to parents. If one of them or both of them attain old age with you, say not "Fie" unto them nor repulse them, but speak unto them a gracious word. And lower unto them the wing of submission through mercy, and say: My Lord! Have mercy on them both, as they did care for me when I was young. [17:23-24]

The recognition and respect of parents is mentioned in the Qur'an eleven times; in every instance, Allah reminds children to recognize and to appreciate the care and love they have received from their parents. In one aspect, Allah demands that children recognize their parents by saying to them:

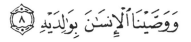

We have enjoined on man kindness to parents. [29:8/46:15]

1. The demand for recognizing parents is made more emphatic when Allah says in the Qur'an Surah Al-Baqarah (The Cow) the following:

وَإِذْ

أَخَذْنَا مِيثَاقَ بَنِىٓ إِسْرَٰٓءِيلَ لَا تَعْبُدُونَ إِلَّا ٱللَّهَ وَبِٱلْوَٰلِدَيْنِ
إِحْسَانًا

*And (remember) when We made a covenant
with the children of Israel, (saying):
worship none save Allah (only), and be
good to parents... [2:83]*

2. In Surah Al-Nisaa' (The Women) Allah (swt)
emphasized again that children should be kind to
their parents.

وَٱعْبُدُواْ ٱللَّهَ وَلَا تُشْرِكُواْ بِهِۦ شَيْـًٔا وَبِٱلْوَٰلِدَيْنِ
إِحْسَانًا

*And serve Allah.   Ascribe nothing as
partner unto Him.   (Show) Kindness unto
parents... [4:36]*

3. In Surah Al An'Am (The Cattle), Allah (swt)
reemphasized that people should be kind to their
parents.

قُلْ

تَعَالَوْاْ أَتْلُ مَا حَرَّمَ رَبُّكُمْ عَلَيْكُمْ أَلَّا تُشْرِكُواْ بِهِۦ
شَيْـًٔا وَبِٱلْوَٰلِدَيْنِ إِحْسَانًا

Say: Come, I will recite unto you that which your Lord has made a sacred duty for you; that you ascribe nothing as partner unto Him and that you do good to parents... [6:151]

III. MOTHERS

Although Islam recognized both parents, mothers are given particular gratitude and respect. This attitude of Islam is understood if we realize the hardships and the suffering that mothers experience in their lives.

It was narrated by Abu Hurairah (R) that a man came to the Prophet (pbuh) and asked him, 'Who is to be close to my friendship?' In this regard, Prophet Muhammad (pbuh) said:

Your mother, your mother, your mother, then your father, then the one closest to your kinship, and the one after.

Islam has endorsed respect for parents by their children even if the parents are non-Muslims. If parents strive very hard to convert their children to non-Islamic beliefs, they don't follow them, but they are to be good to them. In this regard, Allah (swt) says in Surah Luqman:

وَوَصَّيْنَا ٱلْإِنسَٰنَ بِوَٰلِدَيْهِ حَمَلَتْهُ أُمُّهُ وَهْنًا عَلَىٰ وَهْنٍ وَفِصَٰلُهُۥ فِى عَامَيْنِ أَنِ ٱشْكُرْ لِى وَلِوَٰلِدَيْكَ إِلَىَّ ٱلْمَصِيرُ ﴿١٤﴾

$$وَإِن جَٰهَدَاكَ عَلَىٰٓ أَن تُشْرِكَ بِى مَا لَيْسَ$$

$$لَكَ بِهِۦ عِلْمٌ فَلَا تُطِعْهُمَا ۖ وَصَاحِبْهُمَا فِى ٱلدُّنْيَا مَعْرُوفًا ۖ$$

$$وَٱتَّبِعْ سَبِيلَ مَنْ أَنَابَ إِلَىَّ ۚ ثُمَّ إِلَىَّ مَرْجِعُكُمْ فَأُنَبِّئُكُم$$

$$بِمَا كُنتُمْ تَعْمَلُونَ ۝$$

And We have enjoined upon man concerning his parents--his mother beareth him in weakness upon weakness, and his weaning is in two years--Give thanks unto Me and unto your parents. Unto Me is the journeying. But if they strive with you to make you ascribe unto Me as partner that of which you have no knowledge, then obey them not. Consort with them in the world kindly, and follow the part of him who repents unto Me. Then unto Me will you return, and I shall tell you what you used to do. [31:14-15]

IV. <u>MORE RESPECT</u>

Islam teaches us that respect for parents comes immediately after praying to Allah and before Jihad (struggle and striving in the way of Allah). In this respect, the Prophet (pbuh) said the following:

" عَنْ أَبِي عَبْدِ الرَّحْمٰنِ بْنِ مَسْعُودٍ رَضِيَ اللّٰهُ عَنْهُ

قَالَ : سَأَلْتُ النَّبِيَّ صَلَّى اللّٰهُ عَلَيْهِ وَسَلَّمَ : أَيُّ الْعَمَلِ

أَحَبُّ إِلَى اللّٰهِ تَعَالَى ؟ قَالَ : الصَّلَاةُ عَلَى وَقْتِهَا ،

62

قُلْتُ : ثُمَّ أَيُّ ؟ قَالَ : بِرُّ الْوَالِدَيْنِ ، قُلْتُ : ثُمَّ أَيُّ
قَالَ : الْجِهَادُ فِيْ سَبِيلِ اللّٰهِ . "

متفق عليه

Narrated by Abi Abder Rahman Abdullah bin
Massoud (May Allah be pleased with him) saying:
"I asked the Prophet (pbuh), "which deed is more
liked by Allah?" He replied, "*Prayers on time.*"
Then I asked, "Which one is next?" He said,
"*Godliness to parents.*" Then I asked, " Then
which one is next?" He said, "*Jihad in the way of
Allah.*"   (Agreed)

In Islam, respect for parents is so great that the child
and his wealth are considered to be the property of the
parents. In this regard, the Prophet (pbuh) said:

عَنْ عَائِشَةَ (رَضِيَ) أَنَّ رَجُلاً أَتَى إِلَى النَّبِيِّ صَلَّى
اللّٰهُ عَلَيْهِ وَسَلَّمَ يُخَاصِمُ أَبَاهُ فِيْ دَيْنٍ عَلَيْهِ ، فَقَالَ لَهُ
النَّبِيُّ صَلَّى اللّٰهُ عَلَيْهِ وَسَلَّمَ : " أَنْتَ وَمَالُكَ لِأَبِيْكَ . "

Narrated by Aisha (May Allah be pleased with her)
that a person came to the Prophet (pbuh) to resolve
his dispute with his father regarding a loan given to
the father. The Prophet (pbuh) said to the person,
You and your wealth are to your father.

V. FINAL REMARKS

We hope and we pray that all of us will respect our parents while they are alive and even after they are dead. You may honor your parents after they died through the following methods:

1. Make daily Du'a' for them

2. Give a charity on their behalf

3. Institute a perpetual charity on their behalf - such as a Masjid, an Islamic Center, an Islamic Library, an Islamic hospital, an orphanage, a senior citizen's home, etc.

4. Perform Hajj on their behalf or ask someone to do so.

5. Read Qur'an on their behalf

6. Distribute Islamic Literature on their behalf

Let us pray to Allah that we will do our best to respect our parents, to honor them, to be kind to them, to help them, and to please them for the love of Allah.

O Allah! Accept our humble prayers and make us obedient servants to you.

O Allah! Help us to be respectful children to our parents. Ameen.

Chapter 6
FAMILY PROBLEMS
CAUSES AND SOLUTIONS

I. INTRODUCTION

Family is the corner stone of society. If a family is disturbed, the whole society will be disturbed. Hence, the functional requirements of a successful and productive society will be mismanaged and disfunctioned.

Allah (swt) has instructed people to live in a functional family. Such a family is built on mutual love, affection, sympathy, concern, mercy and responsibility, etc. All these characteristics are the blessings of Allah on those who deserve to receive those gifts.

Family life is not all the time "honey and sweet". One has to expect difficulties, problems, sorrows, and hardships, in as much as one does expect happiness. It is understood that people are not living in heaven, but on this planet.

Families throughout history had similar situations. Some of them were able to face them and resolve their problems. Others had to have family counseling, and reconciliation. Others had to go to arbitration in order to resolve their problems. Some other families had to go to courts and solve their problems through "Law and Order." Unfortunately, some families resorted to violence and took the Law in their hands. The latter group ended up with miseries beyond control.

In this article, some of the major causes of family problems will be discussed and some solutions to such problems will be presented. In so doing, some members of the society will be helped. Accordingly, a society shall be built on mutual understanding with responsibilities on both parties.

Experience and time teach people how to handle a problem when it is posed to them. Family counseling has become necessary on a daily basis. Problems that one faces, range between:

1. Husband and wife
2. Father and children; and visa versa
3. Mother and children; and visa versa
4. Mother-in-law and daughter-in-law
5. Father-in-law and son-in-law
6. Brothers and sisters
7. Cousins, nephews and nieces
8. Uncles and aunts
9. Brother-in-law with sister-in-law

A series of problems have been seen, some of which were trivial while others were serious. Some of those problems were resolved while others were beyond control. Some religious scholars had to go to courts and face lawyers and judges. They had to explain the Islamic shari'ah and family laws. They had to travel from state-to-state to help families resolve their problems. They were even blamed, accused and insulted. They opened rescue houses for a large number of them. Some of these families were kept for a few weeks in Muslim houses till the problem was resolved.

Family counseling is not a joke. It is not easy; it is very difficult. There is nothing impossible. It works and the rewards from Allah (swt) are plenty. In this article, some of the major problems are discussed and their solutions are presented. We pray to Allah (swt) to accept our humble efforts, and forgive us for our shortcomings.

II. CAUSES OF DISPUTES

There are many reasons as to why problems arise in a family. A family is composed of a husband, wife and children. Grandparents and grandchildren are part of a family. Cousins, nephews, nieces, aunts, uncles are all part of a single family. A problem may happen to anyone and it affects the whole family members.

Some of the major causes of the problems can be enumerated here:

1. Religious Reasons
2. Economic Problems
3. Medical Reasons
4. The Extended Family Members and the In-Laws
5. Ethical Problems
6. Lack of Understanding of Responsibility while asking for Rights and Privileges
7. Social Problems
8. Educations Problems
9. Political Problems
10. Sexual Relationship
11. Foods and Food Habits
12. Others

III. HUSBAND-WIFE RELATIONSHIP

The number of problems between husband and wife are too many to be counted. Some of the major problems in a relationship are listed here:

1. Both husband and wife could be Muslims, from the

same background and from the same country.
They could be relatives to one another. Still they
have problems among them.

2. There are problems between a Muslim husband
    and a non-Muslim wife. This could be due to
    different religions and cultures.

3. A husband could be an immigrant Muslim while
    the wife would be an indigenent non-Muslim who
    accepted Islam either before or after marriage.
    Problems are created among them due to different
    cultures, customs and understanding the
    applications of Islamic teachings.

When a man is to marry a girl, he should recognize the
following:

1. Both are not the same. None should be the
    rubber stamp to the other. They are to
    complement one another.

2. Both have different talents to share and to benefit
    from one another.

3. Both are in need of each other in happiness or in
    distress. Each should look for the needs and
    happiness of the other.

4. One should ask about his/her duties, obligations
    and responsibilities for the other.

5. Relationship of a husband and wife are not built

on logic and common sense, otherwise, both are losers. One plus one (1+1=?) may not be equal to two. It can be any number. The most important issue is to keep the relationship at its best for both.

6. No one is an angel or satan. Each makes mistakes. No one should remind the other about his/her mistakes. When a chapter is over, they should open a new chapter with a new and positive outlook and approach.

IV. PARENTS-CHILDREN RELATIONS

Some children have had to leave their parents' house and sleep on the streets and eat from garbage dumpsters. Others have been taken away to foster homes. Others were taken away out of the country. Some children were taken away by their mothers or fathers against the will of the other parent. Some children were abused by their parents. The reverse is also true. Some parents were abused by their own children. Restraint orders were given to one or both parents by courts, and they were denied to see their children.

In a previous chapter, solutions to such similar problems were discussed and presented. The reader is requested to read chapter four (4).

V. IN-LAWS RELATIONSHIP

In Islam, it is understood that the in-laws are part of the larger family. It is natural that out of love or jealousy, difference of opinions are presented. Ego may play a big role. Disputes may be created. Finally, they may create problems for the new couple and for themselves as well.

If each and everyone understands his duties, obligations and responsibilities; and if each attends to them, there will not be any problems. However, some problems may arise and they can be taken care of easily.

To keep the in-laws together, we may have to do some of the following recommendations:

1. Invite as many relatives as possible to your house and be generous in your hospitality to all of them.

2. Your father-in-law and mother-in-law have to be treated like your own parents: love, respect, obedience, courtesy, etc.

3. Visit all of your in-laws as often as you can. Be generous and take gifts to them.

4. Whoever is in need of financial help, try to be number ONE to help. Your help should be given privately and never, ever made public. Remember! a sadaqa on a relative is considered in the Book of Allah, double sadaqa.

5. If someone refuses to visit you, you try to visit him. Show him the best of what you have. Treat him the way you like to be treated.

VI. RELIGIOUS PROBLEMS

Some times one may find that either the husband or the wife is over zealous in the practice of the teachings of Islam while the other is relaxed or moderate. Each one tries to pull the other towards himself or herself. They forgot that each one is not biologically, mentally and spiritually the same. Both have to realize that each person has his/her degree of tolerance, and has his/her degree of threshold. They must give and take. They have to communicate and to appreciate each other's degree of threshold. None has to push the other towards him/her. Both have to come close towards each other spiritually. By coming close to each other they will be moderate. Islam is the religion of moderation.

The other problem is when the husband or the wife does not pray five times a day regularly. Or even when one of them does not pray at all. In such a case, a problem can be created for them both. Satan finds it easy to penetrate their house and create commotion between them. The Qur'an is very explicit about this situation. Allah (swt) says in Surah Al-Zukhruf (The Ornaments) the following:

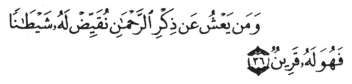

If anyone withdraws himself from remembrance of The Most Gracious, We appoint for him a Satan, to be an intimate companion to him.

(43:36)

Also Allah (swt) says in Surah Taha the following:

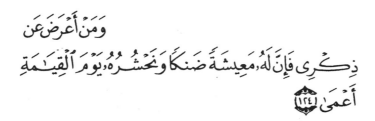

But whosoever turns away from My Message,
verily for him is a life narrowed down, and We
shall raise him up blind on the Day of Judgment.
                                                    (20:124)

The solution of such a problem is that both have to pray regularly, and even in a Jama'ah. If they have children the whole family has an obligation to pray in Jama'ah at least once or twice a day. The rest of the Salat could be prayed individually. The whole family should try to attend Friday Salat and Khutbah so that they will be blessed by Allah.

Anytime Shaitan is to disturb them, they should read Ayah Al-kursi, and the last two Surahs in the Qur'an: "Qul A'uzu". Then and only then, they will be protected by Allah (swt) from Shaitan the sneaker.

VII. ECONOMIC PROBLEMS

It should be understood that almost all of us are to be tested by Allah (swt) in different ways. In Surah Al-Ankabut (The Spider), Allah (swt) says:

$$\text{الٓمٓ ۞ أَحَسِبَ ٱلنَّاسُ أَن يُتْرَكُوٓا۟ أَن يَقُولُوٓا۟ ءَامَنَّا وَهُمْ لَا}$$

$$\text{يُفْتَنُونَ ۞ وَلَقَدْ فَتَنَّا ٱلَّذِينَ مِن قَبْلِهِمْ فَلَيَعْلَمَنَّ ٱللَّهُ ٱلَّذِينَ}$$

$$\text{صَدَقُوا۟ وَلَيَعْلَمَنَّ ٱلْكَٰذِبِينَ ۞}$$

*A. L. M. Do men think that they will be left
alone on saying, "We believe", and that they will
not be tested? We did test those before them and
Allah will Certainly know those who are true and
those who are false.*

(29: 1-3)

At the same time, Allah (swt) reaffirms that He has to
test us in different ways. We should accept the tests and be
patient. Also we should say: "Innaa Lillahi Wa Innaa Ilaihi
Raaji-'oon."

The Qur'an states the following in Surah Al-Baqarah (The
Cow):

$$\text{وَلَنَبْلُوَنَّكُم بِشَىْءٍ مِّنَ ٱلْخَوْفِ وَٱلْجُوعِ}$$

$$\text{وَنَقْصٍ مِّنَ ٱلْأَمْوَٰلِ وَٱلْأَنفُسِ وَٱلثَّمَرَٰتِ وَبَشِّرِ ٱلصَّٰبِرِينَ}$$

$$\text{۞ ٱلَّذِينَ إِذَآ أَصَٰبَتْهُم مُّصِيبَةٌ قَالُوٓا۟ إِنَّا لِلَّهِ وَإِنَّآ إِلَيْهِ رَٰجِعُونَ}$$

$$\text{۞ أُو۟لَٰٓئِكَ عَلَيْهِمْ صَلَوَٰتٌ مِّن رَّبِّهِمْ وَرَحْمَةٌ وَأُو۟لَٰٓئِكَ}$$

$$\text{هُمُ ٱلْمُهْتَدُونَ ۞}$$

*Be sure We shall test you with something of fear
and hunger, some loss in goods, lives and the
fruits (of your toil), but give glad tidings to those
who patiently persevere,-*

*Who say, when afflicted with calamity: "To Allah we
belong, and to Him is our return":-*

*They are those on whom (descend) blessings from
their Lord, and Mercy. And they are the ones that
receive guidance. [2:155-157]*

When someone is struck with a calamity of economic
situation, he should not panic. Money comes and money
goes away. As long as one has faith, health, wisdom, time,
efforts and energy, he should not worry at all. Lack of job
and lack of money is a test and a blessing of Allah (swt)
upon people. One may not know the wisdom till later. A
better job with a better income could be waiting for the
person being tested. One has to make special Salat of
Haajah (need and necessity). At the same time, one has to
make the following Du'a':

*O Allah! saffice me from Your Halal sources, and
not from Haram. Also O Allah! enrich me from
Your provisions but not from anyone else.*

The second Du'a' is the one that Prophet Muhammad
(pbuh) gave to Abu Umamah. The companion had so many
debts and loans and he could not pay them. He was
depressed, distressed and had sorrows. The Du'a' is as
follows:

O Allah! I seek refuge in You from depression and sorrows....

I seek refuge in You from being handicapped and from laziness...

I seek refuge in You from cowardness and stinginess..... and I seek refuge in You (YA Allah!) from debts to overcome me, and from people who destroy me.

The Companion of the Prophet started reading it daily. Allah (swt) opened the door of money and he took care of him. He paid all his debts.

VIII. FINAL REMARKS

In writing about "Family Problems", Causes and Solutions", there are too many to be counted. Problems may be different from place to place and from generation to generation. Many people think that their problem is the only one in the world. They may think that their problem is too difficult to be resolved. Most of the time, their problem is so trivial to be mentioned or to be discussed, and so easy to resolve. It needs a third party who is neutral and objective.

Islam demands the in-laws from both parties to come forward and resolve the problem of the young family. In Surah Al-Nisa' (The women) Allah (swt) says the following:

76

وَإِنْ خِفْتُمْ شِقَاقَ بَيْنِهِمَا فَابْعَثُوا حَكَمًا مِّنْ أَهْلِهِ وَحَكَمًا مِّنْ أَهْلِهَا إِن يُرِيدَا إِصْلَاحًا يُوَفِّقِ اللَّهُ بَيْنَهُمَا إِنَّ اللَّهَ كَانَ عَلِيمًا خَبِيرًا ۝ ٣٥

If you fear a breach between them twain, appoint (two) arbiters, one from his family, and the other from hers; If they seek to set things alright, Allah will cause their reconciliation: For Allah has full knowledge, and is acquainted with all things.

(4:35)

Allah Almighty, God is the Greatest

77

Chapter 7
ADOPTION AND FOSTERING

There is no deity but Allah, and Muhammad is the Messenger of Allah.

I. INTRODUCTION

A serious problem has already spread among Muslims whether they are in minorities or in majorities. This problem is called **adoption** or what is called in Qur'anic language **Tabannee**.

To adopt means to take voluntarily a child of other parents as one's own child. To take by choice into some relationship such as that of an heir, a friend, a citizen, etc.

This problem has somehow spread among Muslims who are in minority because they are influenced by the non-Muslim majority in their own land. The extent of the spread of this problem among Muslims is beyond expectation. The damage of this problem to the family ties, and to the family relations are beyond imagination. The lack of information about Islam, and the history of Islam made the practice of adoption to spread easily among Muslims.

This problem of adoption has also started among Muslims who are in the majority. This is due to the ignorance about Islam as well as the impact of non-Islamic cultures upon the Muslims.

II. QUR'AN ON ADOPTION

Allah has forbidden the method of adoption as being practiced in most parts of the world. Allah (swt) did prohibit Adoption and He wanted us not to change the family names of the children whom they want to help. Allah says in Qur'an in Surah Al-Ahzab about adoption of children the following:

مَا جَعَلَ ٱللَّهُ لِرَجُلٍ مِّن قَلْبَيْنِ فِى
جَوْفِهِۦ ۚ وَمَا جَعَلَ أَزْوَٰجَكُمُ ٱلَّـٰٓـِٔى تُظَٰهِرُونَ مِنْهُنَّ أُمَّهَٰتِكُمْ ۚ
وَمَا جَعَلَ أَدْعِيَآءَكُمْ أَبْنَآءَكُمْ ۚ ذَٰلِكُمْ قَوْلُكُم بِأَفْوَٰهِكُمْ ۖ وَٱللَّهُ
يَقُولُ ٱلْحَقَّ وَهُوَ يَهْدِى ٱلسَّبِيلَ ۝ ٱدْعُوهُمْ لِـَٔابَآئِهِمْ
هُوَ أَقْسَطُ عِندَ ٱللَّهِ ۚ فَإِن لَّمْ تَعْلَمُوٓا۟ ءَابَآءَهُمْ فَإِخْوَٰنُكُمْ
فِى ٱلدِّينِ وَمَوَٰلِيكُمْ ۚ وَلَيْسَ عَلَيْكُمْ جُنَاحٌ فِيمَآ أَخْطَأْتُم
بِهِۦ وَلَٰكِن مَّا تَعَمَّدَتْ قُلُوبُكُمْ ۚ وَكَانَ ٱللَّهُ غَفُورًا رَّحِيمًا
۝ ٱلنَّبِىُّ أَوْلَىٰ بِٱلْمُؤْمِنِينَ مِنْ أَنفُسِهِمْ ۖ وَأَزْوَٰجُهُۥٓ أُمَّهَٰتُهُمْ ۗ
وَأُو۟لُوا۟ ٱلْأَرْحَامِ بَعْضُهُمْ أَوْلَىٰ بِبَعْضٍ فِى كِتَٰبِ ٱللَّهِ
مِنَ ٱلْمُؤْمِنِينَ وَٱلْمُهَٰجِرِينَ إِلَّآ أَن تَفْعَلُوٓا۟ إِلَىٰٓ أَوْلِيَآئِكُم
مَّعْرُوفًا ۚ كَانَ ذَٰلِكَ فِى ٱلْكِتَٰبِ مَسْطُورًا ۝

God has not made for any man two hearts in his (one) body: Nor has He made your wives whom you divorce by Zihar your mothers: Nor has He made your adopted sons your sons. Such is (only) your (manner of) speech by your mouths. But God tells (you) the Truth, and He shows the (Right) way.

Call them by (the names of) their fathers: that is more just in the sight of God. But if you know not their fathers (names, call them) your brothers in faith, or your Maulas. But there is no blame

on you if you make a mistake therein: (what
counts is) the intention of your hearts: and God
is oft-returning, Most Merciful.
The Prophet is closer to the believers than their
own selves, and his wives are their mothers.
Blood-relations among each other have closer
personal ties in the decree of God, (than the
brotherhood) believers and Muhajirs:
Nevertheless do you what is just to your closest
friends: Such is the writing in the Decree (of
Allah). (33:4-6)

III. DISADVANTAGES OF ADOPTION

As we have seen directly from Qur'an, the concept of
adoption is prohibited in Islam. No Muslim has the right to
annex the brotherly relation into the blood relation. The
reason is obvious; one cannot mix two different blood
relations into one. No one can mix the genes of different
people to become of the same family. The wisdom of
prohibition is obvious too: inbreeding is prohibited in Islam
and you may read the details about this prohibition in Surah
Al-Nisa' "The Women".

حُرِّمَتْ عَلَيْكُمْ أُمَّهَـٰتُكُمْ
وَبَنَاتُكُمْ وَأَخَوَاتُكُمْ وَعَمَّـٰتُكُمْ وَخَـٰلَـٰتُكُمْ وَبَنَاتُ
ٱلْأَخِ وَبَنَاتُ ٱلْأُخْتِ وَأُمَّهَـٰتُكُمُ ٱلَّـٰتِىٓ أَرْضَعْنَكُمْ
وَأَخَوَاتُكُم مِّنَ ٱلرَّضَـٰعَةِ وَأُمَّهَـٰتُ نِسَآئِكُمْ

81

وَرَبَـٰٓئِبُكُمُ ٱلَّـٰتِى فِى حُجُورِكُم مِّن نِّسَآئِكُمُ
ٱلَّـٰتِى دَخَلْتُم بِهِنَّ فَإِن لَّمْ تَكُونُوا۟ دَخَلْتُم بِهِنَّ
فَلَا جُنَاحَ عَلَيْكُمْ وَحَلَـٰٓئِلُ أَبْنَآئِكُمُ ٱلَّذِينَ
مِنْ أَصْلَـٰبِكُمْ وَأَن تَجْمَعُوا۟ بَيْنَ ٱلْأُخْتَيْنِ
إِلَّا مَا قَدْ سَلَفَ إِنَّ ٱللَّهَ كَانَ غَفُورًا رَّحِيمًا ﴿٢٣﴾
۞ وَٱلْمُحْصَنَـٰتُ مِنَ ٱلنِّسَآءِ إِلَّا مَا مَلَكَتْ أَيْمَـٰنُكُمْ
كِتَـٰبَ ٱللَّهِ عَلَيْكُمْ وَأُحِلَّ لَكُم مَّا وَرَآءَ ذَٰلِكُمْ أَن تَبْتَغُوا۟
بِأَمْوَٰلِكُم مُّحْصِنِينَ غَيْرَ مُسَـٰفِحِينَ فَمَا ٱسْتَمْتَعْتُم بِهِ
مِنْهُنَّ فَـَٔاتُوهُنَّ أُجُورَهُنَّ فَرِيضَةً وَلَا جُنَاحَ عَلَيْكُمْ
فِيمَا تَرَٰضَيْتُم بِهِۦ مِنۢ بَعْدِ ٱلْفَرِيضَةِ إِنَّ ٱللَّهَ كَانَ عَلِيمًا
حَكِيمًا ﴿٢٤﴾

*Forbidden unto you are your mothers, and your
daughters, and your sisters, and your father's
sisters, and your mother's sisters, and your
brother's daughters and your sister's daughters,
and your milk-mothers, and your milk-sisters,
and your mothers-in-law, and your step-daughters
who are under your protection (born) of your
women unto whom you have gone in- but if you
have not gone in unto them, then it is no sin for
you (to marry their daughters) - and the wives of
your sons who (spring) from your own loins. And
(it is forbidden unto you) that you should have
two sisters together, except what had already*

happened (of that nature) in the past. Lo! Allah is ever-Forgiving, Merciful; And all married women are forbidden unto you save those (captives) whom your right hands possess. It is a decree of Allah for you. Lawful unto you are all beyond those mentioned, so that you seek them with your wealth in honest wedlock, not debauchery. And those of whom you seek content (by marrying them), give unto them their portions as a duty. And there is no sin for you in what you do by mutual agreement after the duty (had been done). Lo! Allah is ever-Knower, Wise.

(4:23-24)

One should not marry his blood relatives or else physical and/or mental malformations do occur. Allah's mercy on us is to protect us and to improve our way of life so as to enjoy it.

Through the method of adoption, the adopted child who lost his family name and his blood relation, may accidentally get married to his own sister without knowledge. Hence, the mental and/or physical malformations may occur. However, for those who would like to do favor by adopting children have to keep the names of the children as they are. In case the progeny of the child is not known, then one has to call them as brothers and sisters-in-Islam, or as Mawlas or Mawali (fostered). They are to be treated as such and they are not blood relatives.

Another disadvantage of adoption is the increase of vices in the societies. The number of the illegitimate children does increase tremendously and the number of crimes resulting from the adoptee children is tremendous.

Adoption could be for infants, children or elderly people. Adoption could be spiritually for any of our ancestors or any Prophet. If adoption is to be accepted, then the best person to be adopted would be Prophet Muhammad (pbuh) as a spiritual father. He would have been called our Father. However, Allah forbade this approach and He insisted that the Prophet is not your adopted father, but he is the Prophet and the Messenger of Allah. In this regard, the Qur'an states emphatically in Surah Al-Ahzab, the following:

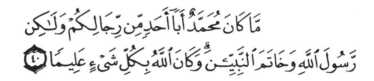

Muhammad is not the father of any of your men, but (He is) the Apostle of God, and the seal of Prophets; and God has full knowledge of all things. (33:40)

IV. PROPHET MUHAMMAD'S ADOPTION

It should be mentioned here that the system of adoption did exist before Islam. Even Prophet Muhammad (pbuh) himself adopted a freed man by the name of Zaid Ibn Haritha as his son. Allah gave a good lesson to mankind in demanding from Prophet Muhammad to marry his cousin Zainab (the wife of the adopted son Zaid). Zaid was asked to divorce his wife Zainab and after the waiting period, the

Prophet was instructed to marry her. In so doing, the concept of Adoption was nullified completely in theory as well as in practice.

In this respect, Allah says in the Qur'an about Muhammad (pbuh) and about the whole story in Surah Al-Ahzab the following:

وَإِذْ تَقُولُ لِلَّذِىٓ أَنْعَمَ ٱللَّهُ عَلَيْهِ وَأَنْعَمْتَ عَلَيْـهِ
أَمْسِكْ عَلَيْكَ زَوْجَكَ وَٱتَّقِ ٱللَّهَ وَتُخْفِى فِى نَفْسِكَ مَاٱللَّهُ
مُبْدِيهِ وَتَخْشَى ٱلنَّاسَ وَٱللَّهُ أَحَقُّ أَن تَخْشَىٰهُ فَلَمَّا قَضَىٰ زَيْدٌ
مِّنْهَا وَطَرًا زَوَّجْنَٰكَهَا لِكَىْ لَا يَكُونَ عَلَى ٱلْمُؤْمِنِينَ حَرَجٌ فِىٓ
أَزْوَٰجِ أَدْعِيَآئِهِمْ إِذَا قَضَوْا مِنْهُنَّ وَطَرًا وَكَانَ أَمْرُ ٱللَّهِ مَفْعُولًا
(٣٧)

Behold! You did say to one who had received the Grace of God and your favor: Retain you (in wedlock) your wife, and fear God. But you did hide in your heart that which God was about to make manifest: You did fear the people, but it is more fitting that you should fear God. Then when Zaid had dissolved (his marriage) with her, with the necessary (formality), we joined her in marriage to you: in order that (in future) there may be no difficulty to the believers in (the matter of) marriage with wives of their adopted sons,

85

when the latter have dissolved with the
necessary (formality their marriage) with
them. And God's command must be fulfilled.
(33:37)

V. <u>FOSTERING</u>

While Allah prohibited the practice of adoption, He mercifully encouraged the practice of fostering. It is well known in the history of Islam that Muslims individually and collectively took care of the orphans. Our beloved Prophet Muhammad (pbuh) was an orphan. His grandfather Abdul Muttalib fostered him. When the grandfather died, his Uncle Abu Talib fostered him in his house along with his twelve children. The Prophet stayed with his Uncle and the family of his Uncle till he got married and settled as an independent family with his wife Khadijah.

In Islam, a fostered child is to be treated as the other children in the house of the foster family. They have to take care of him spiritually, morally, psychologically, economically, educationally, socially and the like. The only thing that such a child is to keep his biological family root and at the same time he cannot inherit from the foster parents as the Islamic Law of Inheritance prescribed. However, the foster parents have the right to make a will to allocate as much as one-third of their properties and estate to the fostered child(ren) if they wish to do so. In so doing, the fostered child will be living and raised in a psychologically, spiritually, socially, economically and culturally stable environment and be a productive citizen in the society.

VI. CONCLUSION

Families throughout the Muslim World have accepted orphans of their kith and kin, or of other families. Foundlings have also been taken care of by special Muslim Institutes. In this way, the communities and the Muslim societies have solved this problem of adoption in the spirit of Islamic teachings. In so doing, they pleased Allah and safeguarded the anticipated problems resulting from the practice of adoption.

I hope and pray that we, as Muslims, will adhere to the teachings of Allah so as to get His pleasure. We hope that we will inform other Muslims about the prohibition of Adoption in Islam. We hope to encourage the practice of fostering in an Islamic way.

O Allah!   Help us, guide us and show us the Straight Path, the path of those whom you have favored from Your Prophets and Messengers.

O Allah!   Make us good and obedient Muslims who are ready to abide by Your teachings.

O Allah!   We have submitted our wills and our totality to you.

O Allah!   Accept us among your obedient servants.
Ameen

Chapter 8
SECURING AN EASY DIVORCE

Allah

I.   INTRODUCTION

Divorce is the most hated thing to Allah. Muslims are ordained to refrain from divorce unless it is the only alternative. Spouses are asked to live peacefully and to look after one another's needs and happiness. If and when there is a problem, the parents of the spouses are to come forward and hash out their differences. The members of the extended families are also to come forward and help the couples to absorb their agonies and to live together peacefully.

To secure a happy marriage, spouses are to know their obligations, duties and responsibilities before they are to ask for their rights.   They are also asked to fulfil these obligations so as to receive rewards and blessings from Allah.

If a divorce has to take place, Muslims should go to a Muslim 'Alim to help them secure an easy way for the divorce without complications. They should make sure that the divorce has to take place according to the teachings of Allah and His Messenger Muhammad (pbuh).

In this chapter the author tries to advise Muslim spouses on how to reduce their problems while dissolving their matrimonial life.

II. A LOSING BATTLE

It should be noted here that those who wish to divorce are the losers while the lawyers and the courts are the winners. The spouses are losers by paying most of their earnings to the court. They are to spend most of their precious time going back and forth to the court. They will spend their happy hours in agony, anxiety and worries. Instead of speaking good words, they are to speak bad words against one another. Their wealth is to be spent into many unnecessary areas.

Most important is the problem of the children. Children who used to love both of their parents are now confused as to whom their love should be. The problem of dowry, the problem of custody and the problem of child support, are all to be faced.

Therefore, divorce is a losing venture to each of the parents as well as to the children. The bi-products of divorce is hatred, troubles, kidnapping of children, losing jobs, foreclosure of the houses, and trouble to the society. Crimes, crises, atrocities and hostilities are the results of many of the divorces.

The only ones who are to survive longer and to keep their jobs on are the lawyers, the judges, the sheriff, the psychiatrists and the police personalities.

Divorce is indeed the most hatred activity to Allah, and people should refrain from it unless it is Hell to continue to live together.

III. AN EASY DIVORCE

The easy divorce is the one where both spouses agree to settle their separation in a friendly way. In as much as they got together through love, friendship and good will to one another, they should settle their divorce with common sense, logic and common terms. They should recognize the rights of the others before they ask for their own ones.

In order to do this, they should have a neutral party who would wish the best for all. This neutral party has only the good will. Unfortunately, this person has no power to enforce the agreement, the settlement or even what is right and good to all. He has no legal power, no police help, no court to recognize and no lawyer to agree with him. This situation applies mainly in a non-Muslim society. If divorce is to take place in a Muslim society where the Islamic Shari'ah is applied, the situation would be totally different.

Therefore, the two spouses should overlook their vengeance and talk as matured and grown-up people. They should agree to the neutral party while trying to make separation and settlement.

IV. PRE-MARRIAGE AGREEMENT

In order to reach an easy agreement for settlement, the bride and groom should sign a prenoctural agreement among themselves. Such an agreement if signed and notorized will be executed by the law enforcement body of the government.

The following items of pre-marriage agreement are of a great importance to help the spouses not to divorce. If they have to divorce, they should think twice; and their divorce may take place with the least headache, least expensive, least trouble and least duration of time. On the other hand, while the two spouses are trying to separate, they are to obey the rules and injunctions stipulated by Allah (swt), before they think of the laws of the non-Muslims society such as USA. People should recognize that they are going to die sooner or later. They are to be brought in the Day of Judgement to Allah. There they are to be judged with justice and fairness. No one is going to defend them at all. Therefore, it is better to obey the teachings of Allah (swt) revealed to Prophet Muhammed (pbuh) in the Qur'an.

V. DECLARATION OF THE PRE-MARRIAGE CONTRACT

Spouses should plan in advance how not to divorce, and how to live peacefully after marriage. At the time of performance of Nikah, they make an agreement amongst themselves, in front of witnesses. They should sign such an agreement which has to be notorized. While living a family life, they should be reminded by that agreement.

The following is a proposed agreement that might be useful to be followed. The agreement between the groom and the bride goes as follows:

Allah Has the Power over anything and everything.

PRE - MARRIAGE CONTRACT

We, the undersigned, (Groom) _____

and (Bride) _____ agree on this day

_____ A.H.[3] _____ C.E.[4]

to the following terms between us, so that our marriage will

last forever with happiness:

1. We marry in the name of Allah, the Creator of the Universe

2. Our Marriage shall be according to Islamic Law (Shari'ah)

3. Our living habits (inside and outside the house) shall be according to the teachings of Islam

4. Our Children shall be raised as Muslims

5. Our divorce (if it takes place) shall be according to Islamic teachings

6. The custody of the children shall be according to Islamic teachings

---

[3]AH: After Hijrah or the migration of Prophet Muhammad from Makkah to Madina. It depends on lunar system.

[4]CE: Common Era. It depends on solar systems.

7. The inheritance shall be according to Islamic Jurisprudence

8. The rites of burial shall be according to Islamic rituals

9. If and when a problem would be created between us and/or with others, we shall go to a Muslim Community and religious leader, a Qadi (Judge) a Mufti, an `Alim and/or a Muslim Council of Qada' (Jurisprudence) or a Muslim Council of Arbitration/Reconciliation

10. If by a chance, a non-Muslim Judge or a non-Muslim lawyer is to handle any case of our affairs, they should rule our case(s) according to the teachings of Islam, i.e. they should seek the help, advice and opinion of Muslim religious leaders so that they execute and enforce the teachings of Islam upon us

We, the undersigned, pray to Almighty Allah to help us to honor this contract. We take God, the Creator of the Universe as our Witness. We make this pledge and this agreement in front of the following witnesses:

Groom:_____ Witness:_____

Bride:_____ Witness:_____

Overseeing this contract: _____

Date of this contract: _____

Notarized By:_____

VI. FINAL REMARKS

It should be mentioned here that marriage is sacred in Islam. It is considered as a matter of worship. Also, one has to state here that family is the corner stone of the society.

Islamic teachings have laid down a strong emphasis as to how one can build a good family as a step forward towards buildings a good society.

Islam is a total way of life, and as such, rules and regulations were laid down to establish a happy life within the family structure. At the same time rules and regulations were also laid down if divorce has to take place.

If divorce has to take place, the spouses have a duty as grownup persons to dissolve the matrimonial unity without damage to both of them in matters of money, dignity, chastity, modesty, integrity and the like. If they have to dissolve their unity they should make it the easy way.

If the spouses have children they should secure an easy way for them to continue to live in peace, harmony and happiness without pushing them to become schizophrenics and trouble-makers in the society.

Therefore, the better and the easy way is not to divorce but to stay together and hash-out their differences. They should give and take from each other. They should accommodate and adjust to the needs of each other. Allah (swt) will help them and reward them for being patient towards each other.

Chapter 9
ISLAMIC ARBITRATION

I. AIMS AND OBJECTIVES

The following is some of the aims of the Islamic Arbitration Council of America (IACA):

1. To act as an arbitrator between disputed parties among the Muslims of North America.

2. To help Muslims to be ruled by Muslims in matters of their daily life.

3. To help Muslims to be judged by the Shari'ah of Islam: Mainly the Qur'an and the Sunnah.

4. To try to solve problems of Muslims on an amicable basis without hardship and without loss of much of their fortune through the American courts.

5. To make sure that the problems of Muslims in America will not be exaggerated.

6. To make sure that such a Council will later be recognized by the American Government, as a legitimate body for the Muslims of America.

II. CONDITIONS FOR ARBITRATION

1. Both parties should agree with the members of the Council to reconcile their problem(s).

   a) A written agreement is to be signed by both parties under disputation.

97

2. Both parties are to present their grievances to the members of the Council.

   a) A written statement is to be presented by both parties independently to the Council.

   b) After receiving the written statement, a meeting is to be called to hear their grievances separately.

   c) Another meeting is to be called to hear their grievances while both of the disputed parties are in the same meeting.

3. Cross Examination, and clarification of the previous meeting is to take place by the Council member.

4. A negotiation of settlement is to be offered by the Council to the disputed parties.

5. A bond is to be paid by each party of about $500 to be in escrow: This money might have to be used as a separate account for expenses of Council activities.

6. The decision of the Council should be binding on both parties.

7. An agreement in writing should be signed by the disputed parties that they will abide by the decision of the Council.

8. An agreement in writing by the disputed parties that

they will refrain from going to a non-Muslim court.

9. A written agreement from the disputed parties that they will not sue the members of the Council for whatever decision they make.

10. If the disputed parties have their case pending in a court, they should withdraw their case before the Council can take care of the problem; otherwise it is useless for the Council to be involved.

III. ACTIVITIES

The main activities of the council is arbitration between the following groups:

1. Between husbands and wives

2. Between parents and children

3. Between children of the same or of different families

4. Between employers and employees

5. Between centers' members of Board of Directors/Board of Trustees/and general membership

6. Between Muslim business individuals or Corporation.

7. Between Muslim Organizations.

IV. MEMBERS OF COUNCIL

A. Qualifications

1. Highly qualified Muslims in North America

2. Well known in the service of Islam

3. Well known in serving Muslims and non-Muslims

4. Individuals whose loyalty is not to any organization, to any ethnic background or to any government

5. Knowledgeable in matters of Shari'ah and in matters of American society

B. Number of the Council Members

1. The number of the Council attending the disputed parties should be not less than (3) and no more than (5) on any particular disputed issue.

C. Membership Duration

1. There should be no duration period to serve as members of the Arbitration Council.

2. Their function will continue as members of the Council, even after the problem is resolved.

100

D. Honorarium

  1. They are volunteers for such activities

  2. They are to be paid their actual expenses if and when expenses are incurred.

  3. An honorarium with reasonable amount is to be given to each arbitrator.

E. Liabilities

  1. The members of the Council are not liable for any damage incurred by any of the disputed parties.

  2. Disputed parties have no right to sue any member of the Council for any decision they make.

F. Decisions

  1. The decision of the Council should be unanimous or general consensus.

  2. Their decisions should be binding on the disputed parties

  3. An appeal by either party to the same Council could be made, if more evidence needs to be offered.

  4. If an appeal is to be made by any party because they feel they did not get what they want, another bond of $1,000 is to be paid by that party, and to be put in

escrow: It is to be used for the activities of the Council.

G. Advisors

1. The members of the Council may seek the advice of a Muslim lawyer if he is available in the area.

2. The advice is <u>not</u> binding on any member or party.

3. His advice mainly should be in the area of the American legal system.

4. His advice will help the presentation of the Council decision in a language not to be misunderstood legally.

H. Meetings of the Council

1. If members of the Council are in the region, they could hold their meeting in a convenient place of their locales.

2. They should meet also with the disputed parties to listen to their complaints.

3. They should meet also among themselves before passing their verdict.

4. If they are far from the region, either they are to be invited for a day or two, and/or a conference.

I. Chairman of the Council

There is no permanent member of any Council formed. There is no permanent chairman of any Council formed. The chairman is selected by Council members from within the group itself. His chairmanship is over after the case is over.

But seek, with the (wealth) which Allah has bestowed on you, the Home of the Hereafter, nor forget your portion in this world: but do you good, as Allah has been good to you, and seek not (occasions for) mischief in the land: for Allah loves not those who do mischief. (Qur'an, 28:77)

That man can have nothing but what he strives for.
(Qur'an, 53:39)

To any that desires the tilth of the Hereafter, we give increase in his tilth: and to any that desires the tilth of this world, We grant somewhat thereof, but he has no share or lot in the Hereafter. (Qur'an, 42:20)

Chapter 10
A SUDDEN TRAGEDY IN THE FAMILY

QUR'AN ON TRAGEDIES

Allah (swt) says in Surah Al-Baqar'ah (The Cow) the following:

وَلَنَبْلُوَنَّكُم بِشَيْءٍ مِّنَ الْخَوْفِ وَالْجُوعِ
وَنَقْصٍ مِّنَ الْأَمْوَالِ وَالْأَنفُسِ وَالثَّمَرَاتِ وَبَشِّرِ الصَّابِرِينَ
﴿١٥٥﴾ الَّذِينَ إِذَا أَصَابَتْهُم مُّصِيبَةٌ قَالُوا إِنَّا لِلَّهِ وَإِنَّا إِلَيْهِ رَاجِعُونَ
﴿١٥٦﴾ أُولَـٰئِكَ عَلَيْهِمْ صَلَوَاتٌ مِّن رَّبِّهِمْ وَرَحْمَةٌ وَأُولَـٰئِكَ
هُمُ الْمُهْتَدُونَ ﴿١٥٧﴾

Be sure we shall test you with something of fear, hunger, some loss in goods, lives and the fruits of your toil, but give glad tidings to those who patiently persevere, who say, when afflicted with calamity, "To Allah we belong, and to him is our return".

They are those on whom descent blessings from their Lord and mercy, and they are the ones that receive guidance. (2:155-157)

I. INTRODUCTION

Tragedy is a calamity, a disaster, a dreadful or a fatal event. It can happen to anyone in the society. That event may happen all of a sudden or it takes place through a process. Any tragedy that takes time, people can train themselves to accept it and to absorb it.

In such a tragedy there are family members, and friends who do help in sharing with their feelings and sympathy. They do send their condolence to the bereaved family. They may visit them and talk to them. Such type of caring and sharing does alleviate and reduce the dimension of a tragedy. However, a tragedy that takes place suddenly, the human mind cannot accept it easily. It may lead to another sudden shock, and to another calamity. One has to learn how to accept a calamity or even a sudden calamity.

In this particular chapter, we will discuss some of the major points regarding tragedy of a sudden death that may happen to anyone of us.

II. TERMINOLOGIES

There is a whole series and varieties of tragedies that take place daily to so many people individually and collectively. The following is a partial list of terminologies concerning tragedies mentioned in the Qur'an.

Transliteration	English Meaning	Arabic
1. Ibtilaa'	Tribulation	ابتلاء
2. Museebah	Calamity	مصيبه
3. Fitnah	Tumult	فتن
4. Tamheess	Purging	تمحيص
5. Imtihan	Examination	امتحان
6. Marad	Sickness	مرض
7. Mowt/Wafaat	Death	موت/وفاه
8. Zilzaal	Earthquake	زلزال
9. Toofaan	Flood	طوفان
10. Hareeq	Fire	حريق
11. Khawf	Fear	خوف
12. Joo'	Famine	جوع
13. Jafaaf	Drought	جفاف

III.   TYPES OF TRAGEDIES

Every human being on this planet earth is to be tested by Allah (swt). Qur'an is full of verses about being tested by Allah with different tests. These could be sickness, car accident, death, family, problems, divorce, loss of job, earthquakes, floods, firebrush, plane crash, etc.

Previous nations were tested with different calamities and tragedies. Allah (swt) gave these examples as lessons to us, so that we behave well, and we obey Allah (swt) with

107

honesty and sincerity. Some of those nations mentioned in the Qur'an are the following:

1. People of Prophet Noah: Allah sent them a flood.

2. People of `Aad: Allah sent them prophet Hud. They were arrogant and claimed to be very powerful. They were destroyed with tornadoes and hurricanes for seven nights and eight days.

3. People of Prophet Lot: They were homosexuals. They were advised to change their sexual behavior but refused. Allah sent them an earthquake and then showered them with brimstones from Hell.

4. The Pharohs refused to listen to Prophet Musa and Haroon. Allah (swt) drowned them into the sea.

IV. WISDOMS OF TRAGEDIES

No one knows the exact wisdom of any particular tragedy. However, by reading Qur'an, we are able to know some of those wisdoms. These are to:

1. Remember Allah, more than before.
2. Test our honesty and sincerity with Allah (swt).
3. Test our patience, tolerance, and threshold.
4. Increase our patience and improve its limits.
5. Increase our credits and our rewards with Allah.
6. Improve and elevate our faith (Imam) with Allah.
7. Wipe out our mistakes.
8. Improve our relationship with Allah (swt).

9.   Make more Du`a' and be close to Allah.
10. Remember that there are still less fortunate people than us, who are struck with terminal sicknesses and disease.

In Surah Al-Ankabut (The Spider) Allah (swt) emphasized the idea that each one has to be tested in this life. He wanted to let us know how far we are honest and sincere in our relationship with him. The Qur'an explains this concept as follows:

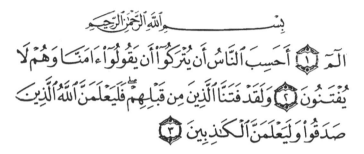

A.L.M. Do men think that they will be left alone on saying "We believe" and that they will not be tested?

We did test those before them, and Allah will certainly know those who are true from those who are false.

(29:1-3)

V.   HANDLING A TRAGEDY

There are a series of methods to be used when a tragedy hits someone. These approaches are complimentary to one another. They are as follows:

1. Having patience (sabr); the rewards of patience is paradise in the Day of Judgement.

2. Remembering Allah (swt) the Creator. You will make Him happy, and in turn He will remember you and He will make you happy.

3. Submitting ourselves to Allah (swt) at the time of tragedy.

4. Saying: Innaa Lillahi... Wa Innaa Ilayhi Raaji-'oon (we came from Allah, and back to Allah we are going)

5. Reading Qur'an and especially Surah Yaseen.

6. Making certain Du`a' for the deceased.

7. Sharing your tragedy with others.

8. Performing extra Salat.

9. Giving Sadaqah (charity) to needy people.

10. Requesting others to make Du`a' for you and for the deceased.

11. Look into his will (Wasiyah) and find out if there is any wish for him before being buried. If there is anything in his will which is contrary to the teachings of Islam, you are not to fulfil such a will.

12. Find out about his debts and loans. Make sure to pay

them as soon as possible. You are responsible in the Book of Allah to take care of them.

13. The body should be buried as soon as possible. The burial should be in the same neighborhood. Shipping the body overseas is not acceptable.

14. Burial rites are to be performed: washing (Ghusl), Kaffan, Salat Janazah, Talqeen, Du'a' and burial.

15. Embalming or cremation are not acceptable in Islam.

16. To bring people on the third day or the seventh day to read Qur'an is not found in the teachings of Islam. Anniversaries of the deceased are not from the Sunnah of the Prophet. Those who insist to observe these occasions as a religious duty and obligation are indeed committing innovation (Bid'ah) in Islam.

VI. AN EXAMPLE OF A CONDOLENCE

The condolence to be given to the bereaved family is as follows:

1. Prepare yourself as to you will say and how you will say.

2. Try to pick up certain verses from Qur'an, and several Ahadith to be quoted and to be told to the family about death.

3. Go back to books of Seerah and Fiqh, and read the chapters on sickness and death.

4. Think it over before you call the family; ask yourself how I am going to sound when I start talking to them to give them condolence.

5. Narrate to them a few verses from Qur'an and a few Ahadith from the Prophet.

6. Make (Du'a' Maghfirah) supplication of forgiveness for the deceased.

7. Mention to them the mobility of the dead person when he was alive, i.e.. The good things he used to do.

8. Say: قَالُوٓاْ إِنَّا لِلَّهِ وَ إِنَّآ إِلَيْهِ رَٰجِعُونَ

    (a) Inna Lillochi was Inna Ilaihi Raji-'oon. (we are from Allah, and to Allah we are coming back)

    (b) La Hawla Wa La Quwata Illa Billah...

    (c) Humuss - Saabiqoon Wa Nahnul Laa-Hiqoon (They are the fore-runners, and we are next to follow)

VII. WISH OF A DECEASED

If you yourself (the reader) is to be the deceased person, what would you wish to say to your family and to the ones who read your message. The following is a partial list of the wish of a deceased to the members of his family and to his friends:

1. Please, my loving family! don't cry or scream. Don't

112

question the wisdom of Allah in making me to die. He knows what He is doing.

2.   Remember! I can still hear and see. Therefore, try to close my eyes immediately.

3.   Don't put me on life support, instead read Surah Yaseen. Allah will either revive me, or make me to die peacefully.

4.   Please try to bury me as soon as possible. Don't put me in the hospital, and if I am to be taken to the hospital, they should not put my body in a freezer. I should be released immediately for burial.

5.   Make sure I won't be cremated or even embalmed.

6.   Don't take me to a mortuary, instead take me to Masjid where the Ghussl, Wudu', Kaffan, and Salat Janazah will be performed on me.

7.   Make sure to read my will before you bury me. Try your best to execute my decisions and recommendations as long as they are according to Islamic Shari'ah.

8.   Look into my debts and my loans. Please try your best to take care of them as soon as possible.

9.   Inform my friends and relatives of my death. Request them to make Du'a' of forgiveness to me.

10.   Inform them about the place of burial and the time for

Salatal Janazah and the time of burial.

11. Donate my clothing to needy individuals.

12. Request the Imam while to perform Salutul Janazah, he is to give a Khutbah about the meaning of death.

13. At the time of bringing me into the grave, request the Imam to make Talqeen to me. Let him request all the visitors to forgive me and to make special Du'a' of forgiveness to me.

14. Before burial make sure no one will open the coffin to expose my face to the public.

15. Tell them after putting me into the grave, whoever can stay longer is better for me. The angels at that time will be asking me. I do need some Du'a' of forgiveness at that time.

16. If a mark is to be put on the grave, make it very simple. Don't use the name of Allah on the mark.

17. It would be a good idea to visit my grave off and on, and make special Du'a' for me.

18. Whenever you make your daily salat remember me in your Du'a' of forgiveness.

19. Whenever you make donations remember me. Try to donate on my behalf for building any masjid, school, hospital, orphanage, etc.

20.　　If my wife wishes to marry after my death, she has to wait for four months and ten days as the Qur'an stipulates.

21.　　If I die in a different country, let the local Muslims there take care of my body to be buried in that part of the world. I should not be brought back to the country of my residence.

22.　　My best wish is to die in Makkah or Madinah. And my wish is to be buried in Jannat Al-Baqee' in the City of Prophet Muhammad (pbuh).

23.　　Please! make sure that my neighbors around my grave should be among the honest, sincere and true Muslim believers. Good neighbors around my grave will improve my next life.

VIII. <u>PATIENCE DUE TO DEATH</u>

A. General

Every person is to tested by Allah (S.W.T.) in this world. There are a whole series of tests, turmoils, sicknesses, accidents and other problems that we face regularly on this planet earth. The worst test is death. it is the end of this life and the trasfer of the soul to another life. It is not easy to accept a tragey of death in comparison to other tragedies. The best advice is to try your best to accept such type of a calamity and be patient.

For those who are tested and are patietn, they are to be rewarded by Allah in this world and in the hereafter.

B. Rewards of Patience

For those who are patient during a clamity, their rewards from Allah (S.W.T.) are tremendous. Some of the rewards are as follows:

1. Salat of Allah (S.W.T.) unto the patient individual. This means that Allah will give that person forgiveness.

2. Mercy (Rahmah): When Allah (S.W.T.) gives someone his mercy, He will let him enter paradise with his mercy. The deeds of a person will not be enough to make him enter paradise without the Mercy of Allah.

3. Guidance (Hidayah) from Allah. A person will be guided by Allah (S.W.T.) in this world till he meets Him in the Day of Judgements. The above three benefits are found in the following verses in Surah Al-Baqarah (The Cow):

وَلَنَبْلُوَنَّكُم بِشَىْءٍ مِّنَ ٱلْخَوْفِ وَٱلْجُوعِ
وَنَقْصٍ مِّنَ ٱلْأَمْوَٰلِ وَٱلْأَنفُسِ وَٱلثَّمَرَٰتِ وَبَشِّرِ ٱلصَّٰبِرِينَ
﴿١٥٥﴾ ٱلَّذِينَ إِذَآ أَصَٰبَتْهُم مُّصِيبَةٌ قَالُوٓا۟ إِنَّا لِلَّهِ وَإِنَّآ إِلَيْهِ رَٰجِعُونَ
﴿١٥٦﴾ أُو۟لَٰٓئِكَ عَلَيْهِمْ صَلَوَٰتٌ مِّن رَّبِّهِمْ وَرَحْمَةٌ وَأُو۟لَٰٓئِكَ
هُمُ ٱلْمُهْتَدُونَ ﴿١٥٧﴾ ۞

Be sure we shall test you. With something of fear and hunger, some loss In goods or lives or the fruits (Of your toil), but give Glad tidings to those Who patiently persevere Who say, when afflicted With calamity: "To Allah We belong, and to Him Is our return" They are those on whom (Descend) blessings from their Lord, And mercy, And they are the ones That receive guidance. (2:155-157)

4. Paradise is the reward for those who practice patience. In Al-Insan (Mankind), Allah (swt) say the following:

وَجَزَىٰهُم بِمَا صَبَرُواْ جَنَّةً وَحَرِيرًا ﴿١٢﴾ مُّتَّكِئِينَ فِيهَا عَلَى ٱلْأَرَآئِكِ لَا يَرَوْنَ فِيهَا شَمْسًا وَلَا زَمْهَرِيرًا ﴿١٣﴾ وَدَانِيَةً عَلَيْهِمْ ظِلَٰلُهَا وَذُلِّلَتْ قُطُوفُهَا تَذْلِيلًا ﴿١٤﴾ وَيُطَافُ عَلَيْهِم بِـَٔانِيَةٍ مِّن فِضَّةٍ وَأَكْوَابٍ كَانَتْ قَوَارِيرَا۠ ﴿١٥﴾ قَوَارِيرَ مِن فِضَّةٍ قَدَّرُوهَا تَقْدِيرًا ﴿١٦﴾ وَيُسْقَوْنَ فِيهَا كَأْسًا كَانَ مِزَاجُهَا زَنجَبِيلًا ﴿١٧﴾ عَيْنًا فِيهَا تُسَمَّىٰ سَلْسَبِيلًا ﴿١٨﴾ ۞ وَيَطُوفُ عَلَيْهِمْ وِلْدَٰنٌ مُّخَلَّدُونَ إِذَا رَأَيْتَهُمْ حَسِبْتَهُمْ لُؤْلُؤًا مَّنثُورًا ﴿١٩﴾ وَإِذَا رَأَيْتَ ثَمَّ رَأَيْتَ نَعِيمًا وَمُلْكًا كَبِيرًا ﴿٢٠﴾ عَٰلِيَهُمْ ثِيَابُ سُندُسٍ خُضْرٌ وَإِسْتَبْرَقٌ وَحُلُّوٓاْ أَسَاوِرَ مِن فِضَّةٍ وَسَقَىٰهُمْ رَبُّهُمْ شَرَابًا طَهُورًا ﴿٢١﴾ إِنَّ هَٰذَا كَانَ لَكُمْ جَزَآءً وَكَانَ سَعْيُكُم مَّشْكُورًا ﴿٢٢﴾

117

And because they were Patient and constant,
He will Reward them with a Garden and
(garments of) silk. Reclining in the (Garden)
On raised thrones, they will see there neither
the sun's (excessive heat) nor (the moon's)
excessive cold. And the shades of the
(Garden) will come low over them, and the
bunches (of fruit), there, will hang low in
humility. And amongst them will be passed
round vessels of silver and goblets of crystal.
Crystal-clear, made of silver: They will
determine the measure thereof (According to
their wishes). And thye will be given to drink
there of a cup (of wine) mixed with Zanjabil.
A fountain there called Salsabil. And round
about them will (serve) youths of perpetual
(freshness): If thou sees them scattereed
pearls. And when thou lookest it is there
thou wilt see a bliss and a realm magnificent.
Upon them will be green garments of fine silk
and heavy brocade, and they will be adorned
with bracelets of silver, and their Lord will
give to them to drink of a wine pure and holy.
"Verily this is a reward for you, an your
endeavour is accepted and
recognized."(Qur'an 76: 12-22)

5.   They will be given all the blessings without being
     accounted for. Allah (swt) says in Surah Al-
     Zumar (The Groups) the following:

Say: "O ye my servants who believe! Fear your Lord. Good is (the reward) for those who do good in this world. ***(Qur'an 39:10)***

6. Allah is with those who are patient. In Surah Prophet Hud, Allah (swt) says the following:

إِلَّا ٱلَّذِينَ صَبَرُواْ وَعَمِلُواْ ٱلصَّٰلِحَٰتِ أُوْلَٰٓئِكَ لَهُم مَّغۡفِرَةٞ وَأَجۡرٞ كَبِيرٞ ﴿١١﴾

Not so do those who show patientce and constancy, and work. Righteousness; for them is forgiveness (of sins) and a great reward. ***(Qur'an 11:11)***

7. They will be rewarded by Allah with the best of what they have achieved in life. In Surah Al-Nahl (The Bees), Allah (swt) says the following:

مَا عِندَكُمۡ يَنفَدُ
وَمَا عِندَ ٱللَّهِ بَاقٖ وَلَنَجۡزِيَنَّ ٱلَّذِينَ صَبَرُوٓاْ أَجۡرَهُم بِأَحۡسَنِ مَا كَانُواْ يَعۡمَلُونَ ﴿٩٦﴾

What is with you must vanish: What is with Allah will endure. And we will certainly bestow, on those who patiently persevere, their reward according to the best of their actions. ***(Qur'an 16:96)***

119

8. They will have in paradise Eternal Homes. In Surah Al-Ra'ad (Thunder) Allah (swt) says the following:

وَٱلَّذِينَ صَبَرُواْ ٱبْتِغَآءَ وَجْهِ رَبِّهِمْ وَأَقَامُواْ ٱلصَّلَوٰةَ وَأَنفَقُواْ مِمَّا رَزَقْنَٰهُمْ سِرًّا وَعَلَانِيَةً وَيَدْرَءُونَ بِٱلْحَسَنَةِ ٱلسَّيِّئَةَ أُوْلَٰئِكَ لَهُمْ عُقْبَى ٱلدَّارِ ﴿٢٢﴾

Those who patiently persevere, seeking the countenance of their Lord; establish regular prayers; spend, out of (the gifts) we have bestowed. Fort their sustenance, secretly and openly; and turn off evil with good: for such there is the final attainment of the (eternal) home. **(Qur'an 13:22)**

9. They will be rewarded by Allah with the best of what they have achieved in life;
(Qur'an 16:96)

10. They are the most successful ones and they will receive the Bliss. **(Qur'an 23:111)**

11. They will be rewarded with the highest place in heaven; and they are to be met with salutations and peace. **(Qur'an 25:75)**

12. They are selected by Allah as leaders to their communities to guide them. **(Qur'an 3:125)**

13. Angels descend unto the Mujahideen who are

120

patient in the battlefield to help them and to give them moral support. *(Qur'an 3:125)*

14.   Allah does help the patient soldiers in the battlefield to win the war against the enemies of Islam. *(Qur'an 8:65)*

C. Examples of patient people

1. The story of the Poetess Al-Khansaa'

Before Islam she lost her brother Sakhr. She wrote the most emotional poem eulogyzing him with weeping and crying. Even her friends who visited her used to cry with her after hearing her poem and her crying voice.

After she accepted Islam, she had four sons. She sent them to the battle of Al-Qadisiyah in Jordan the year 15 A.H. under the leadership of Sa'ad ibn Abi Waqqas and during the caliphate of Umar ibn Alkhaltab. She encouraged them to be steadfast and patient during the battlefield.

All of the four sons were killed in the battlefield. She said: I am honored today that all of them are martyrs. i am patient for their loss; however I pray to Allah to get together with them in paradise.

2. Story of Zan Noon the Egyption

He was performing Tawaf around Ka'abah, and he heard one lady talking to another one about her tragedy. She claimed that her tragedy if being heard by mountain Hunain, the mountain will crack down into pieces. He was shocked and asked her to tell him her story. She said: I had two young sons playing around. One son saw his father making a sacrifice for a lamb. Innocently, that son said to his brother: I want to show you how my father sacrificed the animal. He took his knife and slaughtered his own brother. He was shocked and ran away. When father came, I told him the story. The father went after his son. He found him killed by a lion. When the father tried to come back home, he fell dead due to thirst, sorrows and sun-stroke. She said I want to cry and bring my tears on my face, but my patience makes my heart to cry and to weep rather than my eyes.

3. Story of 'Urwah Ibn Al-Zubair

He had an operation, and the doctor amputated his leg. One friend came to visit him. 'Urwah thought that the friend came to pacify him for the loss of his leg. So 'Urwah told his visitor: If you came to give me condolence for the loss of my leg, I already submitted to Allah with patience to reward me for its loss. The guest told him I came to inform you that your son fell down into a stable and the animals stepped over him and he died one hour ago. 'Urwah said: O Allah! you took one child and left me many... You took one organ from my body and left me many organs... O Allah! You tested me with my body but you were kind to leave me with good health. You tested me with the loss of my son, but you were kind in leaving me the rest of my children.

IX. FINAL REMARKS

A tragedy is a tragedy and it is not easy to be accepted and absorbed without having sorrows and wrong feelings.

One has to recognize that this life is not eternal, but a life of tests and examination. Therefore, one has to expect and accept any decisions made by Allah (swt) against our will or wish. At the same time, one has to plan and prepare himself for the better life to come for him i.e., life after death.

To have a good family and good friends is a blessing from Allah. One should try to do favors to many people. They may in turn make Du'a' of forgiveness (Maghfirah) for him after death. While you are alive try to remember all those relatives who died before you. Make Du'a' for them, and remember their good deeds. Try to forget their bad deeds. Inform the living ones about the good deeds of the deceased before they die.

As long as you have this type of feeling towards the deceased, Allah will inspire other people to do the same for you when you die. As long as you make Allah (swt) happy, he will make you happy in this world, in the grave, in the Day of Assembly, in the Day of Judgement, and on the Sirat Al-Mustaqeem on the way to heaven and paradise.

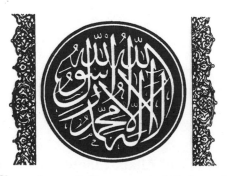

**There is no deity except Allah and
Muhammad is the Messenger of Allah**

Chapter 11
CONDOLENCE MESSAGE

In the Name of Allah, chapter 112 Al-Ikhlas

I. INTRODUCTION

During sad occasions there are no better words than the saying of Allah in the Qur'an, and His Prophet Muhammad, in the Hadith. Allah says in the Surah Al-Baqarah (The Cow) that He is to test us and that we should be patient and steadfast. In this regard, the Qur'an states the following:

وَلَنَبْلُوَنَّكُم بِشَىْءٍ مِّنَ ٱلْخَوْفِ وَٱلْجُوعِ
وَنَقْصٍ مِّنَ ٱلْأَمْوَالِ وَٱلْأَنفُسِ وَٱلثَّمَرَاتِ وَبَشِّرِ ٱلصَّابِرِينَ
ٱلَّذِينَ إِذَآ أَصَابَتْهُم مُّصِيبَةٌ قَالُوٓاْ إِنَّا لِلَّهِ وَإِنَّآ إِلَيْهِ رَاجِعُونَ
أُوْلَٰٓئِكَ عَلَيْهِمْ صَلَوَاتٌ مِّن رَّبِّهِمْ وَرَحْمَةٌ وَأُوْلَٰٓئِكَ
هُمُ ٱلْمُهْتَدُونَ

And surely We shall try you with something of fear and hunger, and loss of wealth and lives and crops; but give glad tidings to the steadfast who say, when a misfortune strike them: Lo! We are Allah's and lo! Unto Him we are returning. Such are they on whom are blessings from their Lord, and mercy. Such are the right guided. [2:155-157]

All of us are to be tested by Allah from the moment we accept to be Muslims; and the more we are close to Allah, the more the tests are to be befallen on us till we meet our Lord. In this respect Allah says in the Qur'an in Surah Al-'Ankaboot (The Spider):

اللَّمَ ﴿١﴾ أَحَسِبَ ٱلنَّاسُ أَن يُتْرَكُوٓا أَن يَقُولُوٓا ءَامَنَّا وَهُمْ لَا
يُفْتَنُونَ ﴿٢﴾

Alif. Lam. Mim. Do people imagine that they will be left (at ease) because they say, we believe, and will not be tested with affliction?

[29:1-2]

At the same time the Prophet (pbuh) said in this regard:

عَنْ أَنَسٍ رَضِيَ اللَّهُ عَنْهُ قَالَ :
قَالَ رَسُولُ اللَّهِ صَلَّى اللَّهُ عَلَيْهِ وَسَلَّمَ : « إِنَّ عِظَمَ
الْجَزَاءِ مَعَ عِظَمِ الْبَلَاءِ ،
وَإِنَّ اللَّهَ تَعَالَى إِذَا أَحَبَّ قَوْمًا ابْتَلَاهُمْ ، فَمَنْ
رَضِيَ فَلَهُ الرِّضَا ، وَمَنْ سَخِطَ فَلَهُ السَّخَطُ » .
رواه الترمذي

It was narrated by Anas (May Allah be pleased with him), that the Messenger of Allah (pbuh) said:

The degree (level) of reward depends upon the degree (gravity) of test, and when Allah Almighty likes a group of people, He tests them; whoever accepts happily, it is to his credit that he will be rewarded; and whoever is disappointed and is unhappy, it is to

126

his discredit and he is to be penlized. [Reported by Tarmazi]

II.   REWARDS OF PATIENCE

If a person is tested with a calamity, and he says:

قَالُوٓاْ إِنَّا لِلَّهِ وَ إِنَّآ إِلَيْهِ رَٰجِعُونَ

Innaa Lillahi Wa innaa Ilayhi Raji-'oon

Allah will give him three types of rewards, namely:

1. Salawat   **Prayers, blessing**

2. Rahmah   **Mercy**

3. Hidayah   **Guidance**

A.   Prayer (Salat)

Concerning the Prayers, Allah and His angels made their prayers unto Prophet Muhammad (pbuh) and therefore He said in the Qur'an about prayer in Surah Al-Ahzab (The Clans):

إِنَّ ٱللَّهَ وَمَلَٰٓئِكَتَهُۥ يُصَلُّونَ عَلَى ٱلنَّبِيِّ يَٰٓأَيُّهَا ٱلَّذِينَ ءَامَنُواْ صَلُّواْ عَلَيْهِ وَسَلِّمُواْ تَسْلِيمًا ٥٦

Lo! Allah and His angels shower blessings on the Prophet. O you who believer! Ask blessings on him and salute him with a worthy salutation. *[33:56]*

This type of special prayer from Allah is to be offered unto those whose are patient when a calamity, a distress, a crisis, a fear, hunger or loss of lives hit them. When Allah gives His prayers on someone, it is the ultimate pacification and satisfaction.

B. Mercy (Rahmah)

Concerning the Mercy of Allah, one has to remember that each one is in need of the Mercy of Allah. We say:

In the name of Allah whose Mercy is maximum and infinite.

We do need the Mercy of Allah in every moment of our life, death, grave, after death and in the Day of Judgement. Without the Mercy of Allah we would be at a loss. Hence the Mercy of Allah will be with those who are patient when a calamity hits them.

C. Guidance (Hidayah)

Concerning the Guidance of Allah, one has to remember that the Hidayah or guidance of Allah will be with those who are patient. We read daily in Surah Al-Fatihah (The Opening):

Show us the straight path (أَهْدِنَا ٱلصِّرَٰطَ ٱلْمُسْتَقِيمَ), i.e., we do ask Allah His Hidayah. However, this Hidayah will be with those who are patient when a calamity hits them.

So, in saying: **Innaa Lillahi Wa Inna Ilayhi Raji-'oon,** one shall receive the best rewards that Allah gives at one time: Prayers, Mercy, Guidance.

Moreover Allah will reward those who are patient with a maximum reward. In this regard Allah said in the Qur'an in Surah Al-Zumar (The Troops):

قُلْ يَٰعِبَادِ ٱلَّذِينَ
ءَامَنُوا۟ ٱتَّقُوا۟ رَبَّكُمْ لِلَّذِينَ أَحْسَنُوا۟ فِى هَٰذِهِ ٱلدُّنْيَا حَسَنَةٌ
وَأَرْضُ ٱللَّهِ وَٰسِعَةٌ إِنَّمَا يُوَفَّى ٱلصَّٰبِرُونَ أَجْرَهُم بِغَيْرِ حِسَابٍ ﴿١٠﴾

...Verily the steadfast (patients) will be paid their wages without stint. [39:10]

Allah asks the believers to be patient and He reminded them that their daily prayers will help them to be patient and steadfast. In this regard, Allah says in the Qur'an in Surah Al-Baqarah (The Cow):

يَٰٓأَيُّهَا ٱلَّذِينَ
ءَامَنُوا۟ ٱسْتَعِينُوا۟ بِٱلصَّبْرِ وَٱلصَّلَوٰةِ إِنَّ ٱللَّهَ مَعَ ٱلصَّٰبِرِينَ ﴿١٥٣﴾

O you who believe! Seek help in steadfastness and prayer. Lo! Allah is with the steadfast. [2:153]

III. DEATH IS A FACT

In a sad occasion. one has to remember that everyone of us is going to die sooner or later. Prophet Muhammad died and it was a shock to his followers. Allah addressed Muhammad (pbuh) by saying to him in Surah Al-Zumar (The Troops):

$$\text{إِنَّكَ مَيِّتٌ وَإِنَّهُم مَّيِّتُونَ}$$

Lo! You will die, and lo! they will die.   [39:30]

Allah also reminded us by mentioning that Prophet Muhammad is no more than a messenger to deliver the message of Allah and that he las to die. He asked the believers not to turn away form Allah. In thus regard, Allah said in Surah Al-'Imran (The Family):

$$\text{وَمَا مُحَمَّدٌ}$$
$$\text{إِلَّا رَسُولٌ قَدْ خَلَتْ مِن قَبْلِهِ الرُّسُلُ أَفَإِين مَّاتَ أَوْ قُتِلَ}$$
$$\text{انقَلَبْتُمْ عَلَىٰ أَعْقَابِكُمْ وَمَن يَنقَلِبْ عَلَىٰ عَقِبَيْهِ فَلَن يَضُرَّ}$$
$$\text{اللَّهَ شَيْئًا وَسَيَجْزِى اللَّهُ الشَّاكِرِينَ ١٤٤}$$

Muhammad is but a Messenger; Messenger (the like of whom) have passed away before him. Will it be that, when he dies or is slain, you will turn back on your heels? He who turns back does no harm to Allah, and Allah will reward the thankful.   [3:144]

130

One has to remember that all of us are going to die even if we are protected by every possible means: physically, biologically, politically, or militarily. Remember what Allah says in the Qur'an in Surah An-Nisa' (The Women):

أَيْنَمَا تَكُونُوا۟ يُدْرِككُّمُ ٱلْمَوْتُ وَلَوْ كُنتُمْ فِى بُرُوجٍ مُّشَيَّدَةٍ وَإِن تُصِبْهُمْ حَسَنَةٌ يَقُولُوا۟ هَٰذِهِۦ مِنْ عِندِ ٱللَّهِ وَإِن تُصِبْهُمْ سَيِّئَةٌ يَقُولُوا۟ هَٰذِهِۦ مِنْ عِندِكَ قُلْ كُلٌّ مِّنْ عِندِ ٱللَّهِ فَمَالِ هَٰٓؤُلَآءِ ٱلْقَوْمِ لَا يَكَادُونَ يَفْقَهُونَ حَدِيثًا ٧٨

Wheresoever you may be, death will overtake you, even though you were in lofty towers...

[4:78]

IV. MORE REWARDS

In such calamities we have to be patient. And as such remember what the Prophet (pbuh) said about the reward for those who are patient, and especially when they are hit with a crisis or a calamity. He said:

عن أبي هريرة رضي الله عنه أن رسول الله ـ صلى الله عليه وسلم قال : " يَقُولُ اللهُ تَعَالَى مَا لِعَبْدِيَ المُؤْمِنِ عِنْدِي جَزَاءٌ إِذَا قَبَضْتُ صَفِيَّهُ مِنْ أَهْلِ الدُّنْيَا ثُمَّ احْتَسَبَهُ إِلاَّ الجَنَّـــةَ "

رواه البخـــــارى

It was narrated by Abu Hurairah (May All be

131

pleased with him) that the Prophet (pbuh) said: *Allah Almighty says that My believing creature has paradise when I take a loving member of his family, and he is patient.*
[Reported by Bukhari]

The Prophet (pbuh) also said:

عَنْ أَبِي هُرَيْرَةَ رَضِيَ اللَّهُ عَنْهُ قَالَ :
قَالَ رَسُولُ اللَّهِ صَلَّى اللَّهُ عَلَيْهِ وَسَلَّمَ :
مَا يَزَالُ الْبَلاءُ بِالْمُؤْمِنِ وَالْمُؤْمِنَةِ
فِي نَفْسِهِ وَوَلَدِهِ وَمَالِهِ حَتَّى
يلقى الله تعالى وما عليه خطيئة • رواه الترمذى

It was narrated by Abu Hurairah that the Messenger of Allah (pbuh) said: *The test (from Allah) continues to stay with the believing male and female in himself (herself), in her/her child and in his/her wealth till he/she meets Allah Almighty and has no sin .*
[Tarmazi]

Moreover the Prophet (pbuh) reminded us that whatever happens to a believer, it is to his credit if he is patient. In this regard he said:

عَنْ أَبِي يَحْيَى صُهَيْبِ بْنِ سِنَانٍ رَضِيَ اللَّهُ عَنْهُ قَالَ :
قَالَ رَسُولُ اللَّهِ صَلَّى اللَّهُ عَلَيْهِ وَسَلَّمَ :
• عَجَبًا لِأَمْرِ الْمُؤْمِنِ إِنَّ أَمْرَهُ كُلَّهُ لَهُ خَيْرٌ
وَلَيْسَ ذَلِكَ لِأَحَدٍ إِلاَّ لِلْمُؤْمِنِ : إِنْ أَصَابَتْهُ
سَرَّاءُ شَكَرَ ،فَكَانَ خَيْرًا لَهُ وَإِنْ أَصَابَتْهُ
ضَرَّاءُ صَبَرَ ،فَكَانَ خَيْرًا لَهُ • رواه مسلم

132

It was narrated by Abu Yahya Suhaib Ibn Sinan
(May Allah be pleased with him) that the Messenger
of Allah said:

*It is a strange thing for a believer,
everything is good for him and not to
anyone else other than the believer:
whenever good reaches him, he is thankful
(to Allah); hence he is rewarded; and
whenever he is hit by a calamity, he is
patients and steadfast; hence he rewarded.*

[Muslim]

We have to remember that for every test and for every
crisis, the Muslim is to be rewarded for. In this regard,
Prophet Muhammad (pbuh) said:

عَنْ أَبِي سَعِيدٍ وَأَبِي هُرَيْرَةَ رَضِيَ اللّهُ عَنْهُمَا
عَنِ النَّبِيِّ صَلَّى اللّهُ عَلَيْهِ وَسَلَّمَ قَالَ :

• مَا يُصِيبُ الْمُسْلِمَ مِنْ نَصَبٍ وَلاَ
وَصَبٍ وَلاَ هَمٍّ وَلاَ حَزَنٍ وَلاَ أَذَىً وَلاَ غَمٍّ
حَتَّى الشَّوْكَةَ يُشَاكُهَا إِلاَّ كَفَّرَ اللّهُ بِهَا مِنْ خَطَايَاهُ .

متفق عليه

It was narrated by Abu Said and Abu
Hurairah (May Allah be pleased with them)
that the Messenger of Allah (pbuh) said:
*Whenever a Muslim is afflicted with fatigue,
lasting illness, worry, sadness, harm of
distress, and even when is pricked with a
thorn, Allah will atone his sins and
mistakes.* **[Agreed upon]**

133

V. HISTORICAL EXAMPLES

In sad occasions one has to remember Islamic history and find out how the previous Prophets have react toward any crisis or calamity.   In case of Prophet Muhammad (pbuh) when his son, Ibrahim, was dying, tears from the eyes of the Prophet came down. The story was reported as such:

عَنْ أَنَسٍ رَضِيَ اللَّهُ عَنْهُ أَنَّ رَسُولَ اللَّهِ صَلَّى اللَّهُ عَلَيْهِ وَسَلَّمَ دَخَلَ عَلَى ابْنِهِ إِبْرَاهِيمَ رَضِيَ اللَّهُ عَنْهُ وَهُوَ يَجُودُ بِنَفْسِهِ فَجَعَلَتْ عَيْنَا رَسُولِ اللَّهِ صَلَّى اللهُ عَلَيْهِ وَسَلَّمَ تَذْرُفَانِ . فَقَــــالَ عَبْدُ الرَّحْمَنِ بْنِ عَوْفٍ : وَأَنْتَ يَارَسُولَ اللَّهِ ؟ فَقَالَ : " يَا ابْنَ عَوْفٍ إِنَّهَا رَحْمَةٌ ۰ ثُـــمَّ أَتْبَعَهَا بِأُخْرَى فَقَالَ : " إِنَّ الْعَيْنَ تَدْمَعُ وَالْقَلْبَ يَحْزَنُ ، وَلَا نَقُولُ إِلَّا مَا يُرْضِي رَبَّنَا ، وَإِنَّا لِفِرَاقِكَ يَا إِبْرَاهِيمُ لَمَحْزُونُونَ " رَوَاهُ البُخَارِي

Narrated by Anas (May Allah be pleased with him) that the Messenger of Allah entered the room where his son, Ibrahim, was dying. Tears were shed form the eyes of the Prophet. Abdur Rahman Ibn 'Auf (a companion) asked the Prophet: "Do you do like that, O Prophet of Allah?" The Prophet answered, "O you, Ibn 'Auf, it is a mercy." Then it was repeated and then said, "Indeed

134

*the eye sheds its tears, the heart saddens,
and we can't say but please our Lord, and
we are sad for the departure of you, O
Ibrahim!"* **[Reported by Bukhari]**

In case of Prophet Aiyub (pbuh) it has been reported
by Allah tested him in his wealth, property and in himself
physically and medically. In every case he was patient,
steadfast and obedient to Allah. His reward from Allah
was a special title. In Surah Saad, Allah (swt) says the
following:

وَاذْكُرْعَبْدَنَآ أَيُّوبَ إِذْ نَادَىٰ رَبَّهُۥٓ أَنِّي مَسَّنِيَ ٱلشَّيْطَٰنُ
بِنُصْبٍ وَعَذَابٍ ۞ ٱرْكُضْ بِرِجْلِكَ هَٰذَا مُغْتَسَلٌ بَارِدٌ وَشَرَابٌ ۞
وَوَهَبْنَا لَهُۥٓ أَهْلَهُۥ وَمِثْلَهُم مَّعَهُمْ رَحْمَةً مِّنَّا وَذِكْرَىٰ لِأُوْلِي ٱلْأَلْبَٰبِ
۞ وَخُذْ بِيَدِكَ ضِغْثًا فَٱضْرِب بِّهِۦ وَلَا تَحْنَثْ إِنَّا وَجَدْنَٰهُ صَابِرًا
نِّعْمَ ٱلْعَبْدُ إِنَّهُۥٓ أَوَّابٌ ۞

*"and make mention (O Muhammad) of Our
bondman, Job, when he cried unto his
Lord (saying): Lo! the devil does afflict
me with distress and torment. (And it was
said unto him): Strike the ground with
your foot. This (spring) is a cool bath and
a refreshing drink. And we bestow on him
(again) his household and therewith the
like thereof, a mercy form Us, and a
memorial for men of understanding. And*

(it was said unto him): Take in your hand a branch and smite therewith, and break not your oath. Lo! We found him steadfast, how excellent a slave! Lo! He was ever turning in repentance (to his Lord). "

[38:41- 44]

VI. <u>FINAL REMARKS</u>

Let me encourage you to be patient whenever a calamity hits you. Let me request you to say: **Innaa Lillahi Wa Innaa Ilayhi Raji-'oon,** so that you will be blessed by Allah. Let me request you to make Du'a' for the deceased Muslims. May Allah bless you and may Allah keep us on the straight path of Islam. Ameen. Let us ask Almighty Allah forgiveness.

VII. <u>SUPPLICATION</u>

Abu Hurairah reported God's Messenger as saying, "When you pray over the dead, make a sincere supplication for him. The following supplications have been taken directly from the saying of Prophet Muhammad (pbuh) after being translated.

O Allah! Forgive those of us who are living and those of us who are dead, those of us who are present and those of us who are absent, our young and our old, our male and our female.

O Allah! To whomsoever of us You give life, keep him

faithful to Islam; and Whosoever of us You take in death, take him as a believer.

O Allah! Do not withhold from us the reward of faith, to try us after his death.

O Allah! So and so son/daughter of so and so is in Your protection and in Your nearer presence, so guard him/her from the trial in the grave and the punishment in hell.

O Allah! You are his/her Lord, You did create him/her. You did guide him/her to Islam. You have taken his/her soul, and You know best his/her inner nature and outer aspect. We have come asking forgiveness, so forgive him/her.

O Allah! Make him/her for us a righteous deed which has gone before us, a recompense gone ahead, a treasure and a reward.

O Allah! Forgive him, have mercy upon him, give him peace and absolve him. Receive him with honor and make his grave spacious; wash him with water, snow and hail. Cleanse him from faults as You would cleanse a white garment form impurity. Requite him with an abode more excellent than his abode, with a family better than his family, and with a mate better than his mate. Admit him to the Paradise, and protect him from the torment of the grave and the torment of the Fire.

Chapter 12
ORPHANS

There is no deity except Allah and
Muhammad is the Messenger of Allah

I. INTRODUCTION

This subject is very important in our daily lives. We have to remember that our beloved Prophet Muhammad (pbuh) was an orphan. His father died before his birth and he was taken care of by his grandfather, mother and his nursing mother. Both his grandfather and mother died when he was still a child, and therefore his uncle, Abu Talib, took care of him. We have to remember that Allah (swt) protected him, raised him and trained him properly. In this regard, Allah (swt) says in Surah Al-Duha (The Morning Hours):

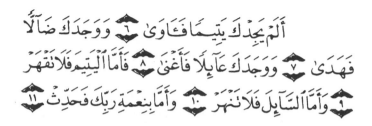

Did He not find you an orphan and give you shelter (and care)? And He found you in need, and made you independent. Therefore, treat not the orphan with harshness, nor repulse the petitioner (unheard); But the Bounty of your Lord rehearse and proclai m!
[93:6-11]

At the same time, Prophet Muhammad (pbuh) said about the One Who took care of him:

Allah trained me and He perfected His training on me.

The UNICEF of United Nations has recognized the rights of the child in November 1959 and the General Assembly of U.N. declared the year of 1979 as the Year of the Child. Islam has already recognized the rights of the child in 1400 years ago, and at the same time, Islam declared the right of the orphans as a complementary decision for the child.

The word 'orphan' has been mentioned in Qur'an twenty-three (23) times in twelve (12) Surahs. The different Qur'anic forms are:

1. Al-yateem   fives times
2. Yateeman   three times
3. Yateemaini   once
4. Al-yatama   fourteen times

As such one does recognize the importance of the orphans in the society, and accordingly one realizes the wisdom of Allah (swt) in mentioning the word 'orphan' 23 times in different contexts in the Qur'an.

II.   TREATMENT

Allah (swt) has ordained us to take care of the orphans in every aspect of our life. Even Allah (swt) asked us to be kind to them. The following is a short summary:

A. **To be kind to the orphan.** The kindness to the orphans was also associated with some other segments of the society, such as: parents, relatives, needy, neighbors, fellow travellers, wayfarers and others. In this regard, Allah (swt) says in Surah An-Nisa (The Women):

$$\cdot \text{وَٱعْبُدُواْ ٱللَّهَ وَلَا تُشْرِكُواْ بِهِۦ شَيْـَٔا ۖ وَبِٱلْوَٰلِدَيْنِ}$$

$$\text{إِحْسَٰنًا وَبِذِى ٱلْقُرْبَىٰ وَٱلْيَتَٰمَىٰ وَٱلْمَسَٰكِينِ وَٱلْجَارِ}$$

$$\text{ذِى ٱلْقُرْبَىٰ وَٱلْجَارِ ٱلْجُنُبِ وَٱلصَّاحِبِ بِٱلْجَنۢبِ}$$

$$\text{وَٱبْنِ ٱلسَّبِيلِ وَمَا مَلَكَتْ أَيْمَٰنُكُمْ ۗ إِنَّ ٱللَّهَ لَا يُحِبُّ مَن}$$

$$\text{كَانَ مُخْتَالًا فَخُورًا ۝}$$

*Serve God, and join not any partners with Him;
and do good - to parents, kinsfolk, orphans, those
in need, neighbors who are near, neighbors who
strangers, the Companion by your side, the
wayfarer (you meet), and what your right hands
posses: for God loves not the arrogant, the
vainglorious.* **[4:36]**

B. **To offer the orphan charity.** This type of a good act
will lead the person to a state of Righteousness **(Birr)**.
The charity should be for the love of Allah (swt), and it
should not be for the sake of fame, reputation or bragging.
Such group of people are considered to be God-fearing
(Muttaqoon).

In this regard Allah (swt) says in Surah Al-Baqarah
(The Cow):

$$\text{۞ لَّيْسَ ٱلْبِرَّ أَن تُوَلُّواْ وُجُوهَكُمْ قِبَلَ ٱلْمَشْرِقِ وَٱلْمَغْرِبِ وَلَٰكِنَّ}$$

$$\text{ٱلْبِرَّ مَنْ ءَامَنَ بِٱللَّهِ وَٱلْيَوْمِ ٱلْأَخِرِ وَٱلْمَلَٰٓئِكَةِ وَٱلْكِتَٰبِ}$$

$$\text{وَٱلنَّبِيِّـۧنَ وَءَاتَى ٱلْمَالَ عَلَىٰ حُبِّهِۦ ذَوِى ٱلْقُرْبَىٰ وَٱلْيَتَٰمَىٰ}$$

141

وَٱلْمَسَكِينَ وَٱبْنَ ٱلسَّبِيلِ وَٱلسَّآئِلِينَ وَفِى ٱلرِّقَابِ وَأَقَامَ
ٱلصَّلَوٰةَ وَءَاتَى ٱلزَّكَوٰةَ وَٱلْمُوفُونَ بِعَهْدِهِمْ إِذَا عَهَدُوا۟
وَٱلصَّبِرِينَ فِى ٱلْبَأْسَآءِ وَٱلضَّرَّآءِ وَحِينَ ٱلْبَأْسِ أُو۟لَٰٓئِكَ ٱلَّذِينَ
صَدَقُوا۟ وَأُو۟لَٰٓئِكَ هُمُ ٱلْمُتَّقُونَ ١٧٧

*It is not righteousness that you turn your faces
towards East or West; but it is righteousness - to
believe in God and the Last Day, and the Angels,
and the Book, and the Messengers; to spend of
your substance, out of love for Him, for your kin,
for orphans, for the needy, for the wayfarer, for
those who ask, and for the ransom of slaves; to be
steadfast in prayer, and practice regular charity;
to fulfill the contracts which you have made; and
be firm and patient, in pain (or suffering) and
adversity, and throughout all periods of panic.
Such are the people of truth, the God-fearing.
[2:177]*

You may also read in Surah Al-Baqarah (The Cow)
(2:215) that we are advised to give charity to orphans
along with parents, kindred, the needy and the wayfarer.

C. **To be just with the orphan.** One has to treat them
nicely, to give them their rights, to feed them properly, to
raise them morally, to help them establish themselves
successfully and to make sure that they are treated justly
in every aspect of life. Prophet Muhammad (pbuh) was
asked about orphans, and Allah (swt) revealed a verse in

142

Surah Al-Baqarah (The Cow) giving them divine guidance as follows:

وَيَسْأَلُونَكَ عَنِ ٱلْيَتَمَىٰ قُلْ إِصْلَاحٌ لَّهُمْ خَيْرٌ وَإِن تُخَالِطُوهُمْ فَإِخْوَٰنُكُمْ وَٱللَّهُ يَعْلَمُ ٱلْمُفْسِدَ مِنَ ٱلْمُصْلِحِ وَلَوْ شَاءَ ٱللَّهُ لَأَعْنَتَكُمْ إِنَّ ٱللَّهَ عَزِيزٌ حَكِيمٌ ﴿٢٢٠﴾

They ask you concerning orphans. Say: "The best thing to do is what is for their good; if you mix their affairs with yours, they are your brethren; but God knows the man who means mischief from the man who means good. And if God had wished, He could have put you into difficulties: He is indeed Exalted in Power, Wise." [2:220]

D. **The female orphans.** They are to be treated kindly and to give them their due rights. Even if one wants to marry the orphan girls, he should be just with them, and he has to give them their rights. Allah (swt) says in Surah An-Nisa (The Women):

وَيَسْتَفْتُونَكَ فِي ٱلنِّسَاءِ قُلِ ٱللَّهُ يُفْتِيكُمْ فِيهِنَّ وَمَا يُتْلَىٰ عَلَيْكُمْ فِي ٱلْكِتَٰبِ فِي يَتَٰمَى ٱلنِّسَاءِ ٱلَّٰتِي لَا تُؤْتُونَهُنَّ مَا كُتِبَ لَهُنَّ وَتَرْغَبُونَ أَن تَنكِحُوهُنَّ وَٱلْمُسْتَضْعَفِينَ مِنَ ٱلْوِلْدَٰنِ وَأَن تَقُومُوا لِلْيَتَٰمَىٰ بِٱلْقِسْطِ وَمَا تَفْعَلُوا مِنْ خَيْرٍ فَإِنَّ ٱللَّهَ كَانَ بِهِۦ عَلِيمًا ﴿١٢٧﴾

143

They ask for your instruction concerning the Women. Say: God does instruct you about them: and (remember) what has been rehearsed unto you in the Book, concerning the orphans of women to whom you give not the portions prescribed, and yet whom you desire to marry, also concerning the children who are weak and oppressed. That you stand firm for justice to orphans. There is not a good deed which you do, but God is well acquainted therewith. [4:127]

E. Orphans have a right from the treasury of the Islamic State. From the revenues of the spoils of wars, orphans are to receive one-fifth of the share as a divine right for them. The other four-fifths of the shares are for Allah (swt) and His Prophet (Islamic State), relatives, the needy and the wayfarer. In this regard Allah (swt) says in Surah Al-Hashr (The Exile).

مَّآ أَفَآءَ ٱللَّهُ عَلَىٰ رَسُولِهِۦ مِنْ أَهْلِ ٱلْقُرَىٰ فَلِلَّهِ وَلِلرَّسُولِ وَلِذِى ٱلْقُرْبَىٰ وَٱلْيَتَـٰمَىٰ وَٱلْمَسَـٰكِينِ وَٱبْنِ ٱلسَّبِيلِ كَىْ لَا يَكُونَ دُولَةًۢ بَيْنَ ٱلْأَغْنِيَآءِ مِنكُمْ وَمَآ ءَاتَىٰكُمُ ٱلرَّسُولُ فَخُذُوهُ وَمَا نَهَىٰكُمْ عَنْهُ فَٱنتَهُوا۟ وَٱتَّقُوا۟ ٱللَّهَ إِنَّ ٱللَّهَ شَدِيدُ ٱلْعِقَابِ ۝

*What God has bestowed on His Apostle (and taken
away) from the people of the township, - belongs
to God - to His Apostle and to kindred and
orphans, the needy and the wayfarer; in order that
it may not (merely) make a circuit between the
wealthy among you. So take what the Apostle
assigns to you, and deny yourselves that which he
witholds from you. And fear God; for God is
strict in Punishment.*   **[59:7]**

One may read also Surah Al-Anfal (The spoils of War)
[8:41]

F. Orphans and Inheritance. As far as their inheritance
is concerned, they are to receive it when they reach the
age of adulthood without being deprived any portion of it.
Allah (swt) asked us not to use it, not to mix it with our
assets and not to eat up their wealth.. If we don't have
enough wealth to raise the orphans, then and only then
may we use as little as possible to raise them. We are to
save their wealth and to invest it in Halal places.
Concerning inheritance Allah (swt) says in Surah An-Nisa'
(The Women):

وَءَاتُواْ الْيَتَٰمَىٰٓ أَمْوَٰلَهُمْ.

وَلَا تَتَبَدَّلُواْ الْخَبِيثَ بِالطَّيِّبِ وَلَا تَأْكُلُوٓاْ أَمْوَٰلَهُمْ إِلَىٰٓ أَمْوَٰلِكُمْ إِنَّهُۥ

كَانَ حُوبًا كَبِيرًا ۝ وَإِنْ خِفْتُمْ أَلَّا تُقْسِطُواْ فِى الْيَتَٰمَىٰ فَٱنكِحُواْ

مَا طَابَ لَكُم مِّنَ النِّسَآءِ مَثْنَىٰ وَثُلَٰثَ وَرُبَٰعَ فَإِنْ خِفْتُمْ أَلَّا تَعْدِلُواْ

فَوَٰحِدَةً أَوْ مَا مَلَكَتْ أَيْمَٰنُكُمْ ذَٰلِكَ أَدْنَىٰٓ أَلَّا تَعُولُواْ ۝

145

To orphans restore their property (when they reach their age), nor substitute (your) worthless things for (their) good ones; and devour not their substance (by mixing it up) with your own. For this is indeed a great sin.

If you fear that you shall not be able to deal justly with the orphans, marry women of your choice, two, or three, or four; but if you fear that you shall not be able to deal justly (with them), then only one, or (a captive) that your right hands possess. That will be more suitable, to prevent you from doing injustice.

[4:2-3]

It should be mentioned here, that it is a big sin to use the wealth of orphans for yourselves and your family. In this regard, Allah (swt) says in Surah An-Nisa' (The Women):

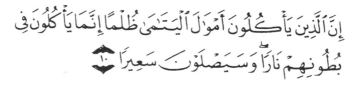

Those who unjustly eat up the property of orphans, eat up a Fire into their own bodies: they will soon be enduring a blazing fire! [4:10]

One may also read Surah Al-An'am (The Cattle) [6:152]; Surah Al-Isra' (The Children of Israel) [17:34] and Surah An-Nisa' (The Women) [4:6,8].

III.   HISTORICAL TREATMENT OF ORPHANS

We have to remember that one of the reasons for the curse of Allah (swt) upon the children of Israel, was because they promised to be kind to orphans and then they forfeited their commitment. In this regard, Allah (swt) reminds us of this story in Surah Al-Baqarah (The Cow) by saying:

وَإِذْ

أَخَذْنَا مِيثَاقَ بَنِى إِسْرَءِيلَ لَا تَعْبُدُونَ إِلَّا اللَّهَ وَبِالْوَالِدَيْنِ
إِحْسَانًا وَذِى الْقُرْبَى وَالْيَتَمَى وَالْمَسَكِينِ وَقُولُوا
لِلنَّاسِ حُسْنًا وَأَقِيمُوا الصَّلَوةَ وَءَاتُوا الزَّكَوةَ ثُمَّ
تَوَلَّيْتُمْ إِلَّا قَلِيلًا مِنكُمْ وَأَنتُم مُّعْرِضُونَ ۞

And remember We took a Covenant from the
Children of Israel (to this effect): Worship none
but God; treat with kindness your parents and
kindred, and orphans and those in need; speak
fair to the people; be steadfast in prayer; and
practice regular charity. Then did you turn back,
except a few among you, and you backslide (even
now).   **[2:83]**

We have to remember that Allah (swt) reminded us of a beautiful story in the Qur'an about Al-Ansar who welcomed Al-Muhajireen. Al-Ansar deprived themselves for the sake of the needy, the orphans and the captives. Allah (swt) says about them in Surah Al-Dahr (Time of Man):

وَيُطْعِمُونَ الطَّعَامَ عَلَى حُبِّهِ مِسْكِينًا
وَيَتِيمًا وَأَسِيرًا ۝ إِنَّمَا نُطْعِمُكُمْ لِوَجْهِ اللَّهِ لَا نُرِيدُ مِنكُمْ جَزَاءً وَلَا شُكُورًا

*And they feed for the love of God, the indigent,
the orphan, and the captive, - (saying), "We feed
you for the sake of God alone: no reward do we
desire from you, nor thanks."* [76:8-9]

Allah (swt) narrated the story of Moses (pbuh) and the
learned person whereby the latter built the wall for the
two orphan boys. There was a treasure beneath the wall
and Allah (swt) wanted to preserve the treasure till they
become adults, so that they will be able to bring out the
treasure. This decision and act was a mercy from Allah
(swt) to the two little orphan boys. In this regard Allah
(swt) said in Surah Al-Kahf (The Cave):

وَأَمَّا الْجِدَارُ فَكَانَ لِغُلَمَيْنِ يَتِيمَيْنِ فِي الْمَدِينَةِ وَكَانَ
تَحْتَهُ كَنزٌ لَّهُمَا وَكَانَ أَبُوهُمَا صَالِحًا فَأَرَادَ رَبُّكَ أَن يَبْلُغَا
أَشُدَّهُمَا وَيَسْتَخْرِجَا كَنزَهُمَا رَحْمَةً مِّن رَّبِّكَ وَمَا فَعَلْتُهُ
عَنْ أَمْرِي ذَلِكَ تَأْوِيلُ مَا لَمْ تَسْطِع عَّلَيْهِ صَبْرًا ۝

*As for the wall, it belonged to two youths,
orphans, in the town; there was, beneath it, a
buried treasure, to which they were entitled;*

148

their father had been a righteous man: so your Lord desired that they should attain their age of full strength and get out their treasure - a mercy (and favor) from their Lord. I did it not of my own accord. Such is the interpretation of (those things) over which you were unable to hold patience. [18:82]

IV. FINAL REMARKS

May I request you kindly to ponder deeply on this subject of orphans and to try your best to do something for these Muslim orphans in the world. May I request you also to discuss this matter with your families today and find out:

1. Who is an orphan among your relatives - friends.

2. Why he/she is orphan. Is it due to a natural catastrope, wars, flood, earthquake or due to a tyrant, a dictator, and an arrogant person in the government.

3. Where are these orphans located?

4. What can I do to alleviate the problem and give them shelter, protection, fostering (not adoption), education, love, affection, monetary support so that they will continue to survive as Muslims and render their services to mankind.

5. Ask yourselves if you were in that position, or if

your child was to be an orphan, what would you like to happen. What would you like to have from those who foster you. Would you want love, affection, sympathy, shelter, moral and spiritual training and education. Don't you want to live honorably as a human being. If you were to be deprived, won't you feel bad about it. Won't you build up a feeling of revenge from the society that you have been raised in.

6. Ask your child whether or not he/she likes to be an orphan. Ask them if they were to be an orphan what would they expect from their relatives, the community, and the government.

7. Finally, you and your family may come up with a logical solution to some of our salient or predominant problems in the society.

If you share your responsibilities in this aspect, I am sure Allah (swt) will be very happy with you, and you will be rewarded in this world and in the hereafter.

Finally, I would like to quote for you what Allah (swt) says in Surah Al-Baqarah (The Cow):

يَسْـَٔلُونَكَ مَاذَا يُنفِقُونَ قُلْ مَآ أَنفَقْتُم مِّنْ خَيْرٍ فَلِلْوَالِدَيْنِ وَٱلْأَقْرَبِينَ وَٱلْيَتَـٰمَىٰ وَٱلْمَسَـٰكِينِ وَٱبْنِ ٱلسَّبِيلِ ۗ وَمَا تَفْعَلُوا۟ مِنْ خَيْرٍ فَإِنَّ ٱللَّهَ بِهِۦ عَلِيمٌ ﴿٢١٥﴾

They ask you what they should spend (in charity).
Say: Whatever you spend that is good, is for
parents and kindred and orphans and those in
want and for wayfarers. And whatever you do
that is good, - Allah knows it well. **[2:215]**

Al-Fatiha or the Opening Chapter
In the Name of Allah,
Most Gracious Most Merciful

Chapter 13
THE ELDERLY

There is no deity except Allah and
Muhammad is the Messenger of Allah

I. INTRODUCTION

The subject of Elderly is very important in every society in the world and especially in the western societies. The elderly are not respected as it should be. Many of them are sent to senior citizen homes instead of keeping them in their own houses or instead of being cared for by their own children. Many of the elderly while in the nursing homes are either killed or attacked by different people. It seems that the elderly are unwanted by the new generation for one reason or another.

This type of life for the elderly is miserable and unbearable. Such type of a situation is considered to be a crisis in the society. It needs to be corrected as soon as possible or else the crisis would lead to a catastrope.

II. ELDERLY CHARACTERISTICS

Islam teaches us to respect the elderly whether they are parents, relatives or any old persons. The word elderly has been used in the Qur'an to mean: Shaikh, Kabeer, 'Ajooz, Arzalil 'Umur, Kibar, etc.

In all those cases, we are informed that the elderly may end up with the following characteristics:

1. Many of them may lose their biological potency.
2. The majority may lose their physical vitality
3. Some of them may lose their mental capacity.
4. A large number of the elderly may increase their emotion feelings beyond limits.

III. BIOLOGICAL ASPECT

As far as the loss of biological potency is concerned, Allah gave us two examples in the Qur'an about Prophet Zakariah and Prophet Ibrahim. Concerning Prophet Zakariah's wife, the Qur'an states the following about her biological impotency in Surah Al- 'Imran (The Family of Imran):

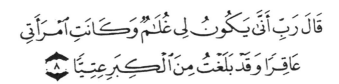

He said: 'O my Lord! How shall I have a son, seeing I am very old, and my wife is barren?' 'Thus,' was the answer, 'Doth God accomplish what He wills.'   [3:40]

While in Surah Mariam, Zakariah is said to have asked the following (in surprise) about getting a child:

He said, 'O my Lord! How shall I have a son, when my wife is barren and I have grown quite decrepit from old age?'   [19:8]

Concerning Prophet Ibrahim, Allah informed us that he was also shocked when he was told about having a child. In

154

Surah Al Hijr (The Rocky Tract) the Qur'an states the following about his biological impotency:

$$قَالَ أَبَشَّرْتُمُونِى عَلَىٰٓ أَن مَّسَّنِىَ ٱلْكِبَرُ فَبِمَ تُبَشِّرُونَ ۝$$

He said: 'Do you give Glad tidings that old age has seized me? Of what, then, is your good news?'

[15:54]

The wife of Prophet Ibrahim was even shocked when she was informed about having a child. She knew that she was an old lady and she could not bear children anymore. In Surah Hud (The Prophet Hud), the Qur'an states the following:

$$قَالَتْ يَٰوَيْلَتَىٰٓ ءَأَلِدُ وَأَنَا۠ عَجُوزٌ وَهَٰذَا بَعْلِى شَيْخًا إِنَّ هَٰذَا لَشَىْءٌ عَجِيبٌ ۝$$

...Seeing I am an old woman, and my husband here is an old man? That would indeed be a wonderful thing!

[11:72]

The wife of Prophet Ibrahim reconfirmed her biological impotency is Surah Al Zariyat (The Winnowing Winds). The Qur'an states the following:

$$فَأَقْبَلَتِ ٱمْرَأَتُهُۥ فِى صَرَّةٍ فَصَكَّتْ وَجْهَهَا وَقَالَتْ عَجُوزٌ عَقِيمٌ$$

155

But his wife came forward laughing aloud:
She smote her forehead and said: A barren
old Woman! [51:29]

IV.   PHYSICAL VITALITY

As far as the loss of physical vitality is concerned, an old person can't do much of the hard work that a young man is able to do. The Qur'an informs us about Prophet Shu'aib who was an old person. He could not do the hard work anymore. His daughters has to take the animals to the spring for water and also to raise them. In Surah Al-Qasas (The Narration), the Qur'an states the following:

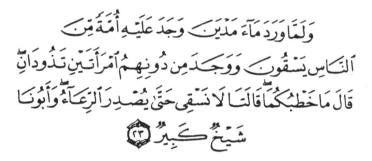

...They said: We cannot water our flocks
until the shepherds take back their flocks:
and our father is a very old man.   [28:23]

The Qur'an also informs us about Prophet Zakariah who admitted his old age and his lack of physical ability. In Surah Mariam, Allah says:

$$\text{قَالَ رَبِّ إِنِّي وَهَنَ ٱلْعَظْمُ}$$

$$\text{مِنِّي وَٱشْتَعَلَ ٱلرَّأْسُ شَيْبًا وَلَمْ أَكُن بِدُعَآئِكَ رَبِّ}$$

$$\text{شَقِيًّا ۞}$$

*Praying: O my Lord! Infirm indeed are my
bones, and the hair of my head does glisten
with grey... [19:4]*

V.   MENTAL CAPACITY

As far as the loss of mental capacity is concerned, Allah
(swt) informs us, in the Qur'an, that any old person may lose
most of his mental capability. Hence he may become senile.
In Surah Al-Hajj (Pilgrimage) and Surah Al-Nahl (The Bee),
Allah (swt) informs us about the senility of the elderly ones.
In Surah Al-Hajj (The Pilgrimage) Allah (swt) says the
following:

$$\text{وَمِنكُم مَّن يُتَوَفَّىٰ}$$

$$\text{وَمِنكُم مَّن يُرَدُّ إِلَىٰ أَرْذَلِ ٱلْعُمُرِ لِكَيْلَا يَعْلَمَ مِنۢ}$$

$$\text{بَعْدِ عِلْمٍ شَيْئًا}$$

*...And some of you are called to die, and some
are sent back to the feeblest old age, so that
they know nothing after having known so
much...*   **[22:55]**

157

VI.   EMOTIONAL FEELINGS

As far as the emotional feelings are concerned, Allah informed us about Prophet Yacoub (Jacob) and his sentimental feelings toward his two last sons: Yusuf and Benjamin. His emotions, his love, his concern, his sympathy, and his sentiments were too high to the extent that he cried and wept extensively until he lost his sight. The climax of this anecdote is summarized in Surah Yusuf as follows:

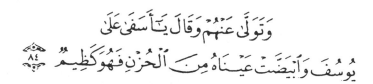

And he turned away from them, and said: how great is my grief for Joseph! And his eyes became white with sorrow, and he fell into silent melancholy.

[12:84]

When he was blamed for his continuous crying :

وَتَوَلَّىٰ عَنْهُمْ وَقَالَ يَا أَسَفَىٰ عَلَىٰ

قَالَ إِنَّمَا أَشْكُوا بَثِّي وَحُزْنِي إِلَى اللَّهِ وَأَعْلَمُ مِنَ اللَّهِ مَا لَا تَعْلَمُونَ ۝

He said: I only complain of my distraction and anguish to God, and I know from God that which you Know not...

[12:86]

158

VII. RESPECT OF ELDERLY

In all these cases we are taught as Muslims, that we should respect the elderly even if they are senile. Our respect to the elderly is more confirmed toward our parents. In Surah Al-Isra' (Night Journey), Allah says to us:

$$۞ وَقَضَىٰ رَبُّكَ أَلَّا تَعْبُدُوٓا۟ إِلَّآ إِيَّاهُ وَبِٱلْوَٰلِدَيْنِ إِحْسَٰنًا ۚ إِمَّا يَبْلُغَنَّ عِندَكَ ٱلْكِبَرَ أَحَدُهُمَآ أَوْ كِلَاهُمَا فَلَا تَقُل لَّهُمَآ أُفٍّ وَلَا تَنْهَرْهُمَا وَقُل لَّهُمَا قَوْلًا كَرِيمًا ٢٣$$

... and that you be kind to parents. Where one or both of them attain old age in your life, say not to them a word of contempt, nor repel them, but address them in terms of honor.   [17:23]

Our beloved Prophet (pbuh) instructed us to respect all those who are old and at the same time we are to have mercy on the young. In one Hadith, it is said:

$$((إِسْتَوْصُوا بِالْكُهُولِ خَيْرًا ، وَارْحَمُوا الشَّبَابْ .))$$

رواه الديلمي

I advise you to be good to the elderly, and to have mercy on the youth.   [El Dailami]

It was reported by Aisha that Prophet (pbuh) instructed us to respect people according to their position. The Arabic text is as follows:

عَنْ عَائِشَةَ رَضِيَ اللّهُ عَنْهَا ، قَالَتْ :
« اَمَرَنَا رَسُولُ اللّهِ صَلّى اللّهُ عَلَيْهِ وَسَلّمَ أَنْ نُنْزِلَ
النَّاسَ مَنَازِلَهُمْ. »

We are informed that any young person who respects the elderly, is to be respected when he becomes old. In one Hadith, the following is reported:

عَنْ أَنَسٍ رَضِيَ اللّهُ عَنْهُ عَنِ النَّبِيّ صَلّى اللّهُ عَلَيْهِ وَسَلّمَ أَنّهُ
قَالَ:
« مَا أَكْرَمَ شَابٌّ شَيْخاً لِسِنَّهِ ، إِلاّ قَيَّضَ اللّهُ لَهُ مَنْ
يُكْرِمُهُ عِنْدَ سِنّهِ. »

Narrated by Anas (May Allah be pleased with him) saying that the Prophet (pbuh) said:

Any young person who is kind to an elderly because of his age, Allah will send him someone who will be kind to him when he becomes old.

[Tarmazi]

In another place, our beloved Prophet (pbuh) denounces the young if they don't respect the elderly in as much as the

160

elderly are denounced if they don't have mercy on the young. the Hadith is as follows:

عَنْ عَمْرُو بن شُعَيْبِ عَنْ أَبِيهِ ، عَنْ جَدّهِ رَضِيَ اللّهُ عَنْهُمْ ، قَالَ:
قَالَ رَسُولُ اللّهِ صَلَّ اللّهُ عَلَيهِ وَسَلَّمَ :
«لَيْسَ مِنَّا مَنْ لَمْ يَرْحَمْ صَغِيرَنَا ، وَ يَعْرِفْ شَرَفَ
كَبِيرِنَا. »

Narrated by 'Amr Ibn Shu'aib through his father and from his grandfather (May Allah be pleased with them), saying that the Messenger of Allah said:

He is not of us, the one who does not have mercy on our young ones, and the one who does not know the respect of our old ones.
[Reported by Dawood & Tarmazi]

The respect that the Prophet (pbuh) instructed us to give to the elderly is also in the field of prayer itself. We are to feel sympathy and concern for the elderly while we are performing the prayer. We should not extend or prolong the congregation prayer especially if there are elderly among the faithful. In one Hadith the Prophet (pbuh) said:

عَنْ أَبِي هُرَيْرَةَ رَضِيَ اللّهُ عَنْهُ انّ النّبِيَّ صَلَّى اللّهُ عَلَيهِ وَسَلّمَ انّهُ
قَالَ :
«إذَا صَلَّى أَحَدُكُمْ بِالنّاسِ فَلْيُخَفِّفْ ، فَإنّ فِيهِمُ
الضَّعِيفَ وَالسَّقِيمَ وَالْكَبِيرَ وَإذَا صَلَّى أَحَدُكُمْ لِنَفْسِهِ فَلْيُطَوِّلْ
مَا شَاءَ. » — متفق عليه —

161

Narrated by Abu Hurairah (May Allah be pleased with him) that the Prophet (pbuh) said:

When a person leads a congregation prayer, let him make it short, as there may be around the weak, the sick and the elderly. However, when a person prays by himself, he may extend his prayer as much as he wishes. [Agreed]

I wish to mention here that Allah Himself gives, among other things, respect to the elderly Muslims. The Prophet (pbuh) says in this regards:

عَنْ أَبِيْ مُوْسَى رَضِيَ اللّٰهُ عَنْهُ، قَالَ رَسُوْلُ اللّٰهِ صَلَّى اللّٰهُ عَلَيْهِ وَسَلَّمَ :
« إِنَّ مِنْ إِجْلَالِ اللّٰهِ تَعَالَى إِكْرَامُ ذِيْ الشَّيْبَةِ المُسْلِمِ ، وَحَامِلُ القُرْآنِ غَيْرِ الغَّالِي فِيهِ ، وَالجَافِيْ عَنْهُ ، وَإِكْرَامُ ذِيْ السُّلْطَانِ المُقْسِطِ. »

رواه ابو داود

Narrated by Abu Musa (May Allah be pleased with him) saying that the Messenger of Allah said:

Among the respect that Allah bestows is to the one who is elderly, gray-haired Muslim, the one who memorized the Qur'an without bragging or deserting it, and the respect to the just ruler.
[Abu Dawood]

162

VIII. FINAL REMARKS

I hope and pray that we Muslims should do our best to respect the elderly and especially our parents. It is a bad habit to send our elderly to senior citizen homes. It is also bad to get rid of our parents and send them to nursing homes. The presence of our parents in our own houses is a blessing from Allah (swt). Their presence will bring peace, happiness, concord, tranquility, mercy and reward from Allah. We should try our best to request our parents to stay with us at our own houses so as to receive the blessings of Allah. We should give a good example to the non-Muslim to do the same with their parents. If we take the initiative and practice this good habit in the American society, we will establish a better society where there is no generation gap. There won't be animosity between the young generation towards the elderly. Instead, there will be kindness, respect, sympathy, concern, and love toward one another. We feel sorry for the elderly who are living in nursing homes, that they are not wanted in the society, that they are deserted, and that arson is committed on them to get rid of them. Poor are the elderly in this society! Many of them are being attack while walking on the streets, robbed and killed. Others are killed while asleep in the nursing homes. Still others are strangled for no reason.

I want you to think seriously about yourself when you will be old. Think seriously abut what is going to happen to you in this part of the world when you will become a senior citizen. I am sure none of us want to be deserted, unwanted or to be thrown away in those nursing homes. None of us want to think that he is a liability when he still an asset to the society.

I wish to request that you visit some of the nursing homes and see for yourselves the life habitat of the elderly. Try to see the type of treatment they receive, the type of food they eat, the type of atmosphere they live in, and the type of feeling they have. Many of us will run away from those places. However, if anyone wishes to live in the open society, he will not feel safe either. We hope and pray, that we will do something good as of today to improve the situation. Once it was said:

$$\text{((عَامِلِ النَّاسَ بِمَا تُحِبُّ أَنْ يُعَامِلُوكَ بِهِ))}$$

Treat people the way you like to be treated.

Also it was once said: $$\text{((كَمَا تُدِينُ تُدَانُ))}$$

The way you treat people, you will be treated.

Let me end this chapter with this Hadith:

$$\text{((لَوْلاَ شُيُوخٌ رُكَّعٌ، وَأَطْفَالٌ رُضَّعٌ، وَشَبَابٌ هُجَّعٌ، لَهَلَكَ النَّاسُ))}$$

Were it not for the elderly who are praying, were it not for the nursing infants, and were it not for the youth who are praying night Tahajud, people would have been destroyed.

Let us pray that Allah guide us to the straight path. Let us ask Allah's guidance and forgiveness. Ameen.

164

Chapter 14
NEIGHBOR

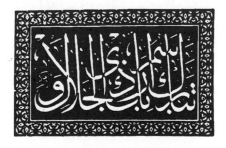

Blessed be the name of your Lord,
full of Majesty, Bounty and Honor.
[Qur'an, 55:78]

I. INTRODUCTION

My talk to you is about NEIGHBOR. This subject is very important anywhere in the world. If one has to live in peace and harmony in his house, he should find out the best neighbor in a good neighborhood and in a good society.

Allah informed us that neighbors are important segments in the society. Without having good neighbors, people will have a difficult and a miserable life. Accordingly Allah (swt) informed us to look after the neighbors, to take care of them, to keep good relations and to make sure that we have good neighbors. In taking care of neighbors, Allah (swt) associated them with categories of parents, relatives, orphans, poor and needy. In Surah An-Nisa' (The Women) Allah says:

وَٱعْبُدُوا ٱللَّهَ وَلَا تُشْرِكُوا بِهِۦ شَيْـًٔا وَبِٱلْوَٰلِدَيْنِ
إِحْسَٰنًا وَبِذِى ٱلْقُرْبَىٰ وَٱلْيَتَٰمَىٰ وَٱلْمَسَٰكِينِ وَٱلْجَارِ
ذِى ٱلْقُرْبَىٰ وَٱلْجَارِ ٱلْجُنُبِ وَٱلصَّاحِبِ بِٱلْجَنۢبِ
وَٱبْنِ ٱلسَّبِيلِ وَمَا مَلَكَتْ أَيْمَٰنُكُمْ إِنَّ ٱللَّهَ لَا يُحِبُّ مَن
كَانَ مُخْتَالًا فَخُورًا ﴿٣٦﴾

Serve God, and join not any partners with Him; and do good -- to parents, kinsfolk, orphans, those in need, neighbors who are near, neighbors who are strangers, the companion by your side, the way-farer (you

166

meet), and what your right hands posses: for
God loves not the arrogant, the vainglorious.

[4:36]

In this Ayah, Allah (swt) categorized for us three types of neighbors that we should take care of . They are:

1. A relative neighbor
2. A strange fellow neighbor
3. A friend Neighbor

All of these neighbors and any Muslim or non-Muslim neighbor is to be taken care of in the best form and in the best manner.

II.   NEIGHBOR CARING

Our beloved Prophet (pbuh) explained to us how to take care of our neighbors. He also insisted that we should do every possible means to make our neighbors happy and satisfied. In one Hadith, the Prophet (pbuh) says:

عَنِ ابْنِ عُمَرَ وَعَائِشَةَ رَضِيَ اللّٰهُ عَنْهُمَا قَالاَ : قَالَ رَسُوْلُ اللّٰهِ صَلّٰى اللّٰهُ عَلَيْهِ وَسَلَّمَ :
«مَازَالَ جِبْرِيْلُ يُوصِيْنِيْ بِالْجَارِ حَتّٰى ظَنَنْتُ أَنَّهُ سَيُوَرِّثُهُ» ــ متفق عليه ــ

Narrated by Ibn Umar and Aisha (May Allah be pleased with them) saying that the Messenger of Allah said:

*Angel Jibril advised me continuously to
take care of the neighbor till I thought
that Allah is to make him an inheritor.*

In another Hadith, the Prophet (pbuh) informed us that
the best person is the one who is good to his neighbors. The
Hadith is as follows:

عَنْ عَبْدِ اللّٰهِ بْنِ عُمَرَ رَضِيَ اللّٰهُ عَنْهُمَا قَالَ : قَالَ رَسُولُ اللّٰهِ
صَلّى اللّٰهُ عَلَيهِ وَسَلّمَ:

« خَيْرُ الْأَصْحَابِ عِنْدَ اللّٰهِ تَعَالَى خَيْرُهُمْ لِصَاحِبِهِ، وَخَيْرُ
الْجِيرَانِ عِنْدَ اللّٰهِ تَعَالَى خَيْرُهُمْ لِجَارِهِ.»

رواه الترمذي

Narrated by Ibn Umar (May Allah be pleased
with him) that the Prophet (pbuh) said:

*The best friend in the sight of Allah is
the one who is good to his companions;
and the best neighbor in the sight of
Allah is the one who is good to his
neighbors.*   [Tarmazi]

There are still more Ahadith about treating neighbors in
the best way.

1. In one Hadith, the following is reported that we should be
kind to our neighbors:

168

عَنْ أَبِي شُرَيْحٍ الْخُزَاعِيِّ رَضِيَ اللهُ عَنْهُ أَنَّ النَّبِيَّ صَلَّى اللهُ عَلَيهِ
وَسَلَّمَ قَالَ :
«مَنْ كَانَ يُؤْمِنُ بِاللهِ وَالْيَوْمِ الآخِرِ فَلْيُحْسِنْ إِلَى جَارِهِ...»
رواه مسلم

Narrated by Abi Shuraih Al-Khuza'i (May Allah
be pleased with him) that the Prophet (pbuh)
said:

*Whoever believes in Allah and the Day
of Judgement, let him do good to his
neighbor...* [Muslim]

2. In another Hadith, the following reported that we should
let them enjoy the food that we cook:

عَنْ أَبِي ذَرٍّ الْغَفَارِيِّ رَضِيَ اللّهُ عَنْهُ، قَالَ : قَالَ رَسُولُ اللّهِ صَلَّى اللّهُ
عَلَيْهِ وَسَلَّم :
« يَا أَبَاذَرٍّ إِذَا طَبَخْتَ مَرْقَةً فَأَكْثِرْ مَاءَهَا وَتَعَهَّدْ
جِيرَانَكَ. » رواه مسلم

Narrated by Abu Zarr Al-Ghaffari (May Allah
be pleased with him) saying that the Prophet
(pbuh) said:

*O Aba Zarr! Whenever you cook food,
increase its contents, and take care of
your neighbors.*

[Muslim]

169

III. WARNING

Our dear Prophet (pbuh) warned those who do harm to their neighbors. He informed them that they are not believers, that they will be punished, and they will not enter paradise. In one Hadith the following reported:

عَنْ أَبِي هُرَيْرَةَ رَضِيَ اللّٰهُ عَنْهُ عَنِ النَّبِيِّ صَلَّى اللّٰهُ عَلَيْهِ وَسَلَّمَ أَنَّهُ قَالَ :

« لَا يَدْخُلُ الْجَنَّةَ مَنْ لَا يُؤْمِنُ جَارُهُ بَوَائِقَهُ . »

ــ متفق عليه ــ

Narrated by Abu Hurairah (May Allah be pleased with him) saying that the Prophet (pbuh) said:

He will not enter paradise, the one whose neighbor is not safe of him. [Muslim]

In another Hadith the following reported:

عَنْ أَبِي هُرَيْرَةَ رَضِيَ اللّٰهُ عَنْهُ، عَنِ النَّبِيِّ صَلَّى اللّٰهُ عَلَيْهِ وَسَلَّمَ أَنَّهُ قَالَ :

« وَاللّٰهِ لَا يُؤْمِنُ ! وَاللّٰهِ لَا يُؤْمِنُ ! وَاللّٰهِ لَا يُؤْمِنُ ! »

« قِيلَ مَنْ يَا رَسُولَ اللّٰهِ؟ قَالَ : « الَّذِي لَا يَأْمَنُ جَارُهُ بَوَائِقَهُ » ــ متفق عليه ــ

170

Narrated by Abu Hurairah (May Allah be pleased with him) saying that the Prophet (pbuh) said:

In the name of Allah, he is not a believer, In the Name of Allah, he is not a believer, In the Name of Allah, he is not a believer. They asked him, who is he O Messenger of Allah! He said: It is he whose neighbor is not safe of him. [Agreed]

IV. OBLIGATIONS

Because the subject of NEIGHBOR is so important in the sight of Allah (swt) and His Messenger Muhammad (pbuh), I will continue offering you more information about this subject.

1. In one Hadith the Prophet (pbuh) explained the physical limits of neighbors:

«كُلُّ اَرْبَعِيْنَ دَارًا جِيْرَانٌ : مَنْ بَيْنَ يَدَيْهِ وَمَنْ خَلْفَهُ وَعَنْ يَمِينِهِ وَعَنْ شِمَالِهِ.»

الطحـــــاوي

Every forty houses are your neighbors: The ones in front of you, the ones from the back, the ones on the right and the ones on the left.

[Tahhawi]

171

2. In another Hadith the Prophet (pbuh) explains the rights
and obligations toward a neighbor:

« حَقُّ الجَارِ إِنْ مَرِضَ عُدْتَهُ، وإِن مَاتَ شَيَّعْتَهُ، وإِنِ
افْتَقَرَ أَقْرَضْتَهُ ، وإِنْ أَعْوَزَ سَتَرْتَهُ ، وإِنْ أَصَابَهُ خَيْرٌ هَنَّأْتَهُ ، وإِنْ
أَصَابَتْهُ مُصِيبَةٌ عَزَّيْتَهُ ، وَلَا تَرْفَعُ بِنَاءَكَ فَوْقَ بِنَائِهِ فَتَسُدَّ عَلَيْهِ
الرِّيحَ ، وَلَا تُؤْذِهِ بِرِيحِ قِدْرِكَ إِلَّا أَنْ تَغْرِفَ لَهُ مِنْهَا. »

رواه الطبراني

*The rights of the neighbor is that, when he is
sick you visit him; when he dies, you go to his
funeral; when he is poor you lend him
(money); when he is in need you protect him;
when he is in happiness you congratulate
him; when he is struck with a calamity, you
condole him; don't raise your building above
his to cut off the wind from him; don't harm
him with the good smell of your food unless
you let him have part of it.* [Tabarani]

3. In another Hadith, the Prophet (pbuh) explained some of
the causes of happiness to the individuals:

« مِنْ سَعَادَةِ المَرْءِ المُسْلِمِ : الجَارُ الصَّالِحُ وَالْمَنْزِلُ الوَاسِعُ
وَالْمَرْكَبُ الهَنِيءُ. »

رواه أحمد والحاكم

172

Among the happiness of a Muslim is a good neighbor, and wide house, and a relaxing transportation... [Ahmad & Al-Hakim]

4. In another Hadith, the Prophet (pbuh) explained to us how to take care of our neighbors in matters of famine and hunger:

$$ «مَا آمَنَ بِي بَاتَ شَبْعَانَ وَجَارُهُ جَـــــائِعٌ.» $$

البـــزار

He is not believing in me, the one who sleeps full while his neighbor is hungry. [Al-Bazar]

5. In another place it is explained that one has to select among others the good neighbor before he selects the house:

$$ « الجَارُ قَبْلَ الدَّارِ، وَالرَّفِيْقُ قَبْلَ الطَّرِيْقِ، وَالزَّادُ قَبْلَ الرَّحِيْلِ.» $$

الخطيب

Neighbor is before the house, the companion is before travelling, and thefood supply is before departure. [Al-Khatib]

V.   BUILDING A GOOD SOCIETY

We are living in a rat race society. We are living in a society where very few people are concerned for others. We are living in a society where people are killing one another without due respect. We are living in a society where neighbors don't know one another. Neighbors of the same building even may not know one another. People are scared of one another. The rate of crime has increased tremendously. People may see one another being hurt and killed, and their answer would be: "It is not my business to get involved." They may see someone screaming, "Help! Help!" Very few of the pedestrians or watchers may come to help. A neighbor may scream, "Help! Help!". However, very few, if any, may be interested to help. Each one is looking after himself.

If you wish to reduce the rate of crime in the society, Muslims are to establish a neighborhood of themselves; otherwise, they should know their neighbors. They should get together with their neighbors and plan strategies to protect their society, their families and their properties. They are to protect their children from drugs, alcohols, rape, adultery, and other vices in the society. There are enough people from the Silent Majority who would be willing to help and to work together to protect the society from the wrong doers.

VI.   FINAL REMARKS

Let me end this article with this Hadith whereby we are to be good to our neighbors:

عَنْ أَبِي هُرَيْرَةَ رَضِيَ اللَّهُ عَنْهُ اَنَّ رَسُولَ اللَّهِ صَلَّى اللَّهُ عَلَيْهِ
وَسَلَّمَ قَالَ :
« مَنْ كَانَ يُؤْمِنُ بِاللَّهِ وَالْيَوْمِ الآخِرِ فَلَا يُؤْذِ جَارَهُ ، وَمَنْ
كَانَ يُؤْمِنُ بِاللَّهِ وَالْيَوْمِ الآخِرِ فَلْيُكْرِمْ ضَيْفَهُ ، وَمَنْ كَانَ يُؤْمِنُ
بِاللَّهِ وَالْيَوْمِ الآخِرِ فَلْيَقُلْ خَيْرًا أَوْ لِيَسْكُتْ . »

— متفق عليه —

Narrated by Abu Hurairah (May Allah be pleased with him) saying that the Messenger of Allah (pbuh) said:

Whoever believes in Allah and the Day of Judgement should not harm his neighbor; whoever believes in Allah and the Day of Judgement should be generous to his guest, and whoever believes in Allah and the Day of Judgement should say good or keep silent.

[Agreed]

We hope and pray that all of us will try our best to practice these teachings in our private and pubic life. May Allah help us and guide us to the right path. Ameen.

175

Chapter 15
VARIETIES OF TOPICS

Paradise At The Feet Of Mothers

Once it was said: "Mother is an institution by herself and she is a leader-maker." She knows how to mold and train her own children in the best way. She does this better than fathers and better than baby –sitters.

While we celebrate Mother's Day, we should recognize that the mother is the backbone of a stable family and a good society. Mothers in their homes keep the family together. With love, affection, sympathy, mercy, trust, patience, and sacrifice they deserve to be honored and respected by all of us. We salute all those mothers who took care of their children, and raised them with honor and dignity, and trained them to be good leaders in America and the world. We need more mothers in our societies to take care of their own children. None should leave this noble responsibility to someone else.

No other parts of the society can do what a mother can do to her own children. Schools, law enforcement, court decisions, rehabilitation centers or any other organization cannot be equal with the institute of the Mother. It is the mother who conceived and accepted the challenge of pregnancy for nine months. She went through difficulties of morning sickness, labor and childbirth. She nurtured her child with tender care till he/she became a grown up.

Therefore, mothers deserved to be respected not only once a year, but every moment of existence. Every child, young and old, male or female, should salute his/her mother daily for the sacrifices that she undertakes. For these reasons and many more, mothers deserve to be in Paradise; and Paradise is humble enough to make itself under the feet of the mother. "Paradise is at the feet of Mothers".

Dowry In Islam

The Islamic terminology of Dowry also (dowery) is called Mahr. There are rules and regulations for a marriage to be consummated. The husband has to offer his wife two types of dowries: An advanced and a late dowry. The advance dowry is to be given to the wife as a sign of a gift at the time of marriage ceremony (Nikah). It is also considered that the man is going to be responsible for the wife's financial upkeep and needs.

The late dowry is to be given to her during their married life. However, if divorce has to take place from his side, he is still obligated to give her the promised late dowry. If the husband makes the life of his wife miserable so that she may seek divorce, he is still obliged by law to fulfill his promise to pay the late dowry.

The advanced dowry could be money, jewelry and/or estate. The same thing is to be applied for the late dowry. In Islam, the man is responsible for all the financial needs of his wife and children. He is also responsible for her financial needs and living expenses after divorce during the waiting period ('iddah) of three months. Even after 'Iddah period, he is still responsible for financial support on her and the children as long as she does not marry any other person.

_ _ PS: The Islamic Jurisprudence dictates that if a woman gets a divorce she has to wait at least three months ('iddah) before she can marry someone else. This is 'Iddah of divorce. However, if the husband dies, the 'Iddah (waiting period) for the wife is four months and ten days; after which she has the right to marry someone else. By the way! The man has NO 'Iddah (waiting period) whether divorce takes place or the death of the wife.

178

Marrying A non-Muslim

Islam is a universal Religion to all mankind, and it is meant till the Day of Judgment. It deals with spiritual issues, as well as with social, economic, political, educational, and financial issues.

As far as Family situation is concerned, Muslims are encouraged to get married as soon as possible so that the society will stay preserved from any immoral life. The parents of the young couples are to help initially their youth financially, morally, socially and spiritually in order for them to stay good citizens in the country they live in.

Islam has encouraged Muslims to marry from Muslim families. The two families have to accept each other, and to unite together to form a bigger family. However, the teachings of Islam prohibit any Muslim lady to marry a non-Muslim man. There is wisdom behind this type of commandment. If a non-Muslim man wants to marry a Muslim lady, he has to accept Islam faithfully and not superficially. Otherwise, an Imam will not be able to solemnize their marriage.

If the young couple decide to marry in accordance with the Civil Law of the country, their marriage in the Book of God (Allah) is null and void. Their life is considered unacceptable and they live a life of adultery. For this reason, Muslim ladies have to marry Muslim men.

A Muslim man is allowed to marry a lady from the people of the Book (Christians and Jews) under certain conditions. They should be living in a Muslim country whereby the Legislative system, as well as the Legal system and the Executive Power are under the Rules of Islamic Jurisprudence.

179

Children Custody In Islam

The teachings of Islam are very humane. The teachings of Islamic jurisprudence are meant to help people to live in peace, harmony and with fairness and justice. As far as the family in Islam is concerned, Islam insists that people should refrain from divorce. Counseling is a must. Settling problems should be taken care by relatives, otherwise by official people in the government. However, if divorce has to take place, then legal settlement has to be enforced.

As far as the custody of the children is concerned, Islamic Jurisprudence dictates that the mother of the children has their full custody till they reach the age of puberty. The father has the visitation rights.

During the period of custody the husband is obliged to take care of the following:

1. Late dowry has to be paid to the mother of the children.

2. During the three months of 'Iddah (waiting period) he is financially responsible for his divorced wife.

3. After the waiting period, the husband is still obliged to spend on his ex-wife and his children.

4. He is to make sure that they live in a reasonable housing facility. He is to pay all their expenses: food, electricity, education, transportation, clothing, medical expenses, etc.

5. If the mother is nursing her baby, the ex-husband is to spend on the mother extra money; otherwise he is to pay for another woman to nurse the child.

6. If the mother of the children decided to get married after the waiting period ('Iddah), Islam allowed her to do so. However, she will lose her monthly alimony, but the ex-husband is still obliged to take care of the living expenses of the children till they become independent.

7. Visitation of the father has to be agreed upon through court order, mutual agreement, or arbitration. Most likely, the children are to stay with their father, while mother will have the right of visitation.

8. In case the mother cannot handle raising her own children, then the grandmother from the mother side will take care of the children. If she cannot handle them, then any female relative from the mother side such as sister or aunt shall take care of them.

9. In case a female relative from the mother side of the children is to take care of them, the father of those children is still responsible to spend on the foster mother, as well as taking care of the children financially.

10. After the age of puberty, the children are given the choice to decide whether to stay with their mother, or join their father.

11. The responsibility of the father will continue towards his children till they get married, and be on their own.

Chapter 16
RELATIONSHIP

I.   Introduction

The title of this paper may or may not explain the theme for discussion. Many other titles could have been used, but for the sake of modesty and respect to the readers, the author refrained from using other titles. The other subjects could be: The Un-natural Relationships, The Unethical Sex Relations... The Immoral Life Style... The Dirty Sex Relationship... The Filthy Sex Life, and the Precursors of the Destruction of Life on this Planet Earth... To be more specific, the title could be about Homosexuality, Lesbianism, and the transgender.

This subject is very sensitive to talk or to write about. There are people who are for this New Life Style, while others are against it. Society today is already over-exposed to this subject to the extent that people are confused what to do, or what to say. Scientists as well as social workers, and religious leaders are either for or against it. Unfortunately some religious leaders have allowed and accepted that type of life style: 'Don't tell and don't ask' or 'Do what you want as long as you are happy.'

Honest and sincere people are astonished as to what they want to do. They are afraid to speak out. Those who practice the un-natural sex life have become very vocal. They make demonstrations, and they have lawyers to defend them. They also have pseudo-scientists who encourage them to continue to practice their un-natural biological life style. They try to prove to them that such sex relations are natural. It has genetic relationship! There is a gene on the chromosome, which is responsible for such sex indulgence! This means that they put the blame on God who allowed such a gene to be there for such type of sex life style!

This type of approach reminds us about other group of religious hierarchy who claim that every person is born sinful. This means that there is a gene on the chromosome, which is responsible for sins from the day of Adam until the Day of Judgment. There is nothing to wipe out such gene of sin except by believing in Jesus as a son of god or god himself. He is the savior for the original sin. If this is true, then those who are practicing homosexuality and lesbianism should be forgiven for what they do as long as they believe in Jesus as their savior. This means that such life should be considered the natural way of life to live, and people should be encouraged to do so.

If society allows such people to take over, people will be either wiped-out from this planet earth, or they will be extinct. However, they will be affected by a series of diseases first, before they are to be cursed by the Creator. For those who are among the silent majority, they themselves will be cursed first, hit first, and penalized first. To be silent, means those people do agree to what goes on. They are considered "complacent".

II.   Historical Incident

This incident of Homosexuality is not new. It took place in history during the life of Prophet Abraham and Prophet Lot. Such incident took place in North Palestine. For the first time in history, some local people got involved in homosexuality. It was really a strange thing to happen. It was unnatural. People in the neighboring areas could not believe that such type of sex life could exist.

The Most Merciful God Almighty (Allah) sent them Prophet Lot to guide them to the healthy life, and to the natural way that they were created. It seems that the local people refused to listen. They insisted to continue such type of sex life. Finally, Allah cursed them, and then He wiped them out totally from this planet earth. He sent them an earthquake. He made sure that all of them were to die. The earth was turned upside down. More so, Allah sent small birds carrying pebbles from Hell Fire. They were showered with such type of pebbles. They were burned into ash. Then Allah showered them with hot salty water from Hell. They vanished completely from this planet earth. The whole area became The Dead Sea in Palestine. It is left as a lesson to the new generations.

Prophet Lot and the neighboring people with their Prophet Abraham were saved, and all those who followed them. This incident was mentioned several times in the Qur'an. In Surah Hood, Allah (swt) says the following:

فَلَمَّا ذَهَبَ عَنْ إِبْرَاهِيمَ الرَّوْعُ وَجَاءَتْهُ الْبُشْرَى يُجَادِلُنَا فِي قَوْمِ لُوطٍ

إِنَّ إِبْرَاهِيمَ لَحَلِيمٌ أَوَّاهٌ مُنِيبٌ

يَا إِبْرَاهِيمُ أَعْرِضْ عَنْ هَذَا إِنَّهُ قَدْ جَاءَ أَمْرُ رَبِّكَ وَإِنَّهُمْ آتِيهِمْ عَذَابٌ غَيْرُ مَرْدُودٍ

وَلَمَّا جَاءتْ رُسُلُنَا لُوطًا سِيءَ بِهِمْ وَضَاقَ بِهِمْ ذَرْعًا وَقَالَ هَذَا يَوْمٌ عَصِيبٌ

184

وَجَاءَهُ قَوْمُهُ يُهْرَعُونَ إِلَيْهِ وَمِنْ قَبْلُ كَانُوا يَعْمَلُونَ السَّيِّئَاتِ
قَالَ يَا قَوْمِ هَؤُلَاءِ بَنَاتِي هُنَّ أَطْهَرُ لَكُمْ فَاتَّقُوا اللَّهَ وَلَا
تُخْزُونِ فِي ضَيْفِي أَلَيْسَ مِنْكُمْ رَجُلٌ رَشِيدٌ
قَالُوا لَقَدْ عَلِمْتَ مَا لَنَا فِي بَنَاتِكَ مِنْ حَقٍّ وَإِنَّكَ لَتَعْلَمُ مَا نُرِيدُ
قَالَ لَوْ أَنَّ لِي بِكُمْ قُوَّةً أَوْ آوِي إِلَى رُكْنٍ شَدِيدٍ
قَالُوا يَا لُوطُ إِنَّا رُسُلُ رَبِّكَ لَنْ يَصِلُوا إِلَيْكَ فَأَسْرِ بِأَهْلِكَ
بِقِطْعٍ مِنَ اللَّيْلِ وَلَا يَلْتَفِتْ مِنْكُمْ أَحَدٌ إِلَّا امْرَأَتَكَ إِنَّهُ مُصِيبُهَا
مَا أَصَابَهُمْ إِنَّ مَوْعِدَهُمُ الصُّبْحُ أَلَيْسَ الصُّبْحُ بِقَرِيبٍ
فَلَمَّا جَاءَ أَمْرُنَا جَعَلْنَا عَالِيَهَا سَافِلَهَا وَأَمْطَرْنَا عَلَيْهَا حِجَارَةً
مِنْ سِجِّيلٍ مَنْضُودٍ
مُسَوَّمَةً عِنْدَ رَبِّكَ وَمَا هِيَ مِنَ الظَّالِمِينَ بِبَعِيدٍ

When fear had passed from (the mind of) Abraham and the glad tidings had reached him, he began to plead with Us for Lot's people. For Abraham was, without doubt, forbearing (of faults), compassionate, and given to penitence. O Abraham! Seek not this, the decree of your Lord has gone forth: for them there comes a chastisement that cannot be turned back. When our messengers came to Lot, he was grieved on their account and felt himself powerless (to protect) them. He said: "This is a distressful day." And his people came rushing towards him, and they had been long in the habit of practicing abominations. He said: "O my people! Here are my daughters: they are purer for you (if you marry)! Now fear Allah and cover me not with

185

disgrace about my guests! Is there not among you a single right-minded man?" They said: "Well don't you know we have no need of your daughters: Indeed you know it quite well what we want!" He said: "If I had power to suppress you or that I could betake myself to some powerful support." (The Messengers) said: "O Lot! We are Messengers from your Lord! By no means shall they reach you! Now travel with your family while yet a part of the night remains, and let not any of you look back: But your wife (will remain behind): To her will happen what happens to the people. Morning is their time appointed: Is not the morning night? When Our decree issued, We turned (the cities) upside down, and rained down on them brimstones hard as baked clay, spread, layer on layer, marked from your Lord; nor are they ever far from those who do wrong! (11: 74-83)

One may read more about that historical group of people in Qur'an in the following chapters:

No	Name of Surah	English Meaning	Surah/Ayat No.
1.	Surah Al-A'raaf	The Heights	(7: 80-84)
2.	Surah Al-Hijr	The Rocky Tract	(15: 61-75)
3.	Surah Al-Anbiyaa'	The Prophets	(21: 74-75)
4.	Surah Ash-Shu`araa'	The Poets	(26: 160-175)
5.	Surah An-Naml	The Ants	(27:54-58)
6.	Surah Al-`Ankaboot	The Spider	(29: 28-35)
7.	Surah As-Saaffaat	Those Ranged in Ranks	(37: 133-138)
8.	Surah Al-Qamar	The Moon	(54: 33-39)

186

| 9. | Surah At-Tahreem | Holding (something) to be Forbidden | (66: 10) |

III.   Causes Of Homosexuality

There is no scientific proof that homosexuality is caused by a gene on any chromosome. The only hypothesis is **"You are what you eat."** The food chemistry affects the chemistry of the blood, and in turn affects the chemistry of the brain. Finally, the person behaves one way or the other.   There are many experiments conducted on animals as well as on human beings. Scientists using micro and macro elements found out that there are correlation between foods and behavior.

Another fact to mention is that men have more male hormones in their body than female hormones. Therefore, after the age of puberty the secondary appearance will be having beard, hair on body and coarse voice. On the contrary, women have more female hormones than male hormones.   Therefore, after the age of puberty, their secondary appearance is to have soft skin, long hair, breasts, etc.

If a man takes female hormones either by injection or ingestion, his secondary appearance starts to change from a male to a female. The reverse is true for a woman. If she takes male hormones, her secondary appearance will look like a man. The more a person takes a hormone of the other gender, the more that person will look like the other gender. Finally, that person will automatically behave similar to the other gender.

It should be stated here that sex behavior is also influenced by the amount of hormones secreted and excreted into the blood stream. The more a man ingests or injects female sex hormones into his body, the more he feels he is like a woman. His sex appetite would be like a woman, while he is a man. Therefore, his sexual orientation will be shifted toward another man. Many people do not know really why their sexual orientation has been shifted toward the same gender. To explain this type of disorder orientation of sexual behavior, one has to give a specific example. There is a female sex hormone called Diethylstilbestrol (DES). It is given to chicken and steer (beef). The chicken at the age of four weeks looks like eight weeks old. The steer at the age of six months looks like two years old. This means that the animal will grow faster within a short period of time. Therefore, the farmer is benefiting tremendously through the use of DES steroid hormone. The USDA has advised farmers not to use such a hormone, but many farmers still use it. No one can detect the presence of such hormone in the animals. Doctors of Veterinarian Medicine (DVM) would not be able to find out, even when they are trying to supervise the slaughtered animals.

This hormone DES is a steroid hormone. This means that it cannot be destroyed easily by cooking procedures. It stays in the meat. When a man eats meat daily (beef or chicken), he is building in his body more female hormone. His sex orientation will definitely shift toward the same gender.

There are few other causes that lead to homosexuality. Some of which are the following:

1. Ignorance: Many people do not know enough about hormones and their influence on the body.

2. Over-exposure of XXX-rated films or videos.

3. Pornography, topless shows, night clubs, etc.

4. Social life including dancing and drinking.

5. Intimidation by the peers and friends.

6. The easy accessibility of the un-natural life style to public.

7. Lack of committed scholars and religious leaders to advise their own constituents as well as the public in general.

8. The absence of a moral society in public. Those who believe in morality are hiding themselves. They do not feel obliged to educate their people. They are to be cursed by Allah.

9. Lack of role models in public affairs to speak the truth.

10. Lack of disciplinary methods for those who transgress the limits of natural way of life.

11. Lack of true treatment for those who fall into the trap of the un-natural life style.

12. The presence of fake scientists who lie through research by encouraging people to accept the immoral life to be considered a norm of life.

13. Some people want to put the blame on the Creator God, Who created them with a gene which is responsible for such type of relationship. This is not true. God is fair and just. He will

never do such type of mistake and then He is to punish them in similar way as He punished the people of Prophet Lot.

14. A large number of people are not yet aware about the effects of foods and liquids on the metabolic reactions of the body.

15. The same thing could be said about the effects of foods on the behaviors of people: To be hyper or dull, and/or to be active or lazy.

16. Lack of practicing the teachings of God on a daily basis. Any person who declines from obeying what God has revealed, will be a target to Satan. He will be easily swayed from the straight path to the wrong one. One has to remember what Allah (swt) said in Surah Zukhruf (The Ornaments):

وَمَنْ يَعْشُ عَنْ ذِكْرِ الرَّحْمَنِ نُقَيِّضْ لَهُ شَيْطَانًا فَهُوَ لَهُ قَرِينٌ

If anyone withdraws himself from remembrance of (Allah) most Gracious, We appoint for him an evil one, (Shaitan), to be an intimate companion to him. (43: 36)

IV.   Prevention

In order to live in peace and harmony, one has to follow the rules and regulations that the Creator Allah (swt) has laid down. God has already created us with the best shape, the best organs and the best biological systems in our body. He also guided mankind by sending them prophets, messengers, teachers, and faithful scholars. Those who follow His advice, will live a happy life on this planet earth, and will be rewarded paradise in the hereafter.

190

In order to live a righteous life, the following is a partial list of preventive methods that keep people on the right path of Allah:

A. For the Society

1. The government should endorse and enforce family and moral values in the society.

2. Penal systems should be applied on those who go astray from the main streams of morality.

3. Official personnel should abolish all those programs about pornography, vulgarity, immorality and any activity that may lead to such social bad behaviors.

4. The official people in the government such as USDA and FDA should pass a law to stop the use of Diethystibestrol (DES) and Estrogen on animals.

5. People should be educated about the effects of foods on their sexual behavior.

6. The school administrators should re-assess their educational systems and programs. They should stop showing any type of programs that lead to immorality. Their physical education programs should be improved and corrected. They should have separate classes for boys and girls. They should correct the places for dressing, washrooms, and shower areas.

7. People should be informed about the history of previous nations, and especially that group of people during the days of Prophets Abraham and Lot.

8. People should be encouraged to get involved in spirituality within the limits that Allah has prescribed in Qur'an, and the Prophet has explained.

9. Families should encourage their children to get married as soon as possible so as to protect them from getting involved in Haram. They should make the procedures and requirements of marriage easy and the least expensive.

10. People should be encouraged to go to the mosques and benefit from religious and educational programs rather than being isolated.

B. For the Individual

As individuals, the following is a partial list of recommendations to be followed:

1. Each person should make a program for himself to follow the basic teachings of Islam.

2. Try to make sure that you pray on time the five daily prayers, as well as to attend Salatul Jumu'ah.

3. Try to read Qur'an daily and especially at Fajr time.

4. Try to listen to the recitation of Qur'an daily so that you will enjoy the melodic voice and the echo of recitation.

5. Try to eat the right foods, and abstain from the foods that are adulterated with hormones, pesticides, preservatives, and ingredients that might lead to sickness, disease, or that might lead to changing the sexual orientation.

192

6. Try to increase fruits and vegetables as much as possible in your daily diets. On the other side, try to reduce the consumption of meat and meat products.

7. If your sexual orientation is going to change to abnormal behavior, try to fast Mondays and Thursdays as much as possible. In doing so, you will control your lusts, detoxify the poisons in your body, purify your body from foreign hormones, and bring you back to Allah with purity and honesty. As long as you can control your appetite for foods and liquids, you will easily control your sexual relationship. Allah (swt) will send you angels from Heaven to help you to direct you to the right path, and to protect you from all types of satans, demons, and other types of devils.

8. More important of all, you have to wake up before Fajr and pray salatul Haajah as much as possible. It is usually at the time of Sahr whereby Allah (swt) exalts Himself and extends His help to all those who are in trouble.

9. Plan to have spiritual vacation by performing Umurah and Hajj as much as possible.

10. Each one should remember death: we should prepare ourselves to go to the grave. We should remember everything we say or do. We should recognize that there is a Day of Judgment where all of us are going to be brought in front of God to be judged. No one is going to help us or to defend us. Therefore, we should follow the teaching of Allah as much as possible. We should be grateful to Allah for all the benefits that He rendered for us. Ameen.

193

V.   Final Remarks

One has to remember that this life is a life of tests. One has to prepare himself for all varieties of problems. He should try to know the causes; then it will be easy for him to prevent himself from such problems. One should recognize that Allah (swt) tests us with what we like or with what we hate. If He gives us wealth, health and happiness, we should be grateful to Him. However, if He tests us with difficulties, problems, and other calamities, we should be patient. However, we should make sadaqa (charity), and offer special Salatul Haajah. Then Allah (swt) will take care of our problem. He will definitely give us credit for our patience.

Allah (swt) created us to live a life of a human being, with all the necessities of life. We are not angels, and we are not animals, but we join them in certain ways. In both ways there are rules and regulations so that we enjoy life with all its dimensions.

There are rules and regulations for sex relationship even between husband and wife so that they will not get venereal diseases. On the contrary they will get blessings and rewards from Allah. It is up to the individuals, families, societies and governments to adopt and follow the straight path of Allah. Then and only then, they will be blessed by Allah, and they will live in peace and harmony the rest of their life. Moreover, in the Day of Judgment, they will be rewarded with paradise. We pray that people all over the world will work together to prevent the immoral way of life. Ameen.

194

Chapter 17
ISLAMIC FAMILY LAW

United States Department of State
Washington, D.C. 20520 *

DISCLAIMER: THE INFORMATION IN THIS CIRCULAR RELATING TO THE LEGAL REQUIREMENTS OF SPECIFIC FOREIGN COUNTRIES IS OBTAINED FROM PAST EXPERIENCE AND IS NOT NECESSARILY AUTHORITATIVE. QUESTIONS INVOLVING INTERPRETATION OF SPECIFIC FOREIGN LAWS SHOULD BE ADDRESSED TO FOREIGN COUNSEL.

ISLAMIC FAMILY LAW

NOTE:

The information contained in this flyer is intended as an introduction to the basic elements of Islamic law and the terms most frequently encountered in the press and literature of Islamic countries. It is **not** intended as a legal reference.

It is also designed to make clear the basic rights and restrictions resulting from mixed marriages. For Americans the most vexing of these restrictions have been:

-- the inability of wives to leave an Islamic country without permission of their Muslim husbands;

-- the wives inability to take their children from these countries without such permission; and

-- the fact that fathers have ultimate custody of children.

- - - * This information is important to Muslim Imams in USA to recognize and realize the different Schools of Thoughts, as well as how each Muslim country applies the Shari'ah of Islam

The law under consideration is Sunni (orthodox). Where particular legal school is not indicated, the legal opinion stated represents the consensus of the four Sunni legal schools.

BACKGROUND

Islamic family law is the collection of those laws upon which the Muslim family is founded and which govern the relationships among its members. Included are laws relating to marriage, children's and other relatives' rights, and the finances of the family, including expenses and the distribution of inheritances and bequests.

In Islamic law (Sharia), the term "family: (usra) includes the husband and wife, the children, the ascendants of the married pair, and all relatives including collateral ones (hawashi) in addition to brothers and sisters. Paternal aunts and uncles and their children belong to the usra, as do maternal uncles and their children.

Islamic family law has retained a sacrosanct status even in states that have secularized many other parts of their legal systems. Three major exceptions are: Turkey, which adopted the Swiss civil code during the reforms of Ataturk; and to lesser extents Tunisia and the People's Democratic Republic of Yemen (South Yemen), where polygamy is prohibited and marriages contracted in violation of reform laws are invalid. Because of the strong hold of the tradition on family law, reformers, instead of seeking to change family law radically, have generally attempted to modify or restrict traditional practices to provide legal safeguards for those parts of classical Islamic family law honored more in the breach than in

196

practice. The latter consideration has been particularly important in the case of women's rights.

MARRIAGE (NIKAH)

In Islam, the act of marriage occurs with the conclusion of the marriage contract. The contract is preceded by the betrothal, in which each of the contracting parties seeks to determine if the other is free to marry and the man expresses his desire for the marriage. Because the proposal is not a contract but a promise to make a contract, either party may withdraw from it, thus ensuring complete freedom of choice.

The marriage contract is concluded by an offer (ijab) and acceptance (qabul), both of which must be made on the same occasion (fi majlis wahid) by two qualified parties. Three conditions are necessary to make the marriage valid:

--   there must be nothing in the form or content of the contract indicating that it is intended to be of limited duration.

--   the contract must be made public; and

--   there must be no impediment, either temporary or permanent, caused by various types of relationships that would interdict the marriage.

If a marriage has been contracted by competent persons in the presence of two witnesses and has been adequately publicized, it is complete and binding. It requires no religious or other rites and ceremonies because in Islamic law formalities have no value insofar as contracts are concerned; they are conducted only if both parties are willing.

IMPEDIMENTS

Marriage is permanently prohibited to persons between whom there exist certain relationships that cannot be terminated. These involve blood ties (qaraba), marriage ties (musahara), and milk relationships. Marriage is temporarily prohibited as a result of certain relationships or conditions that can be terminated; the prohibition obtains only as long as the relationship or condition exists.

PERMANENT IMPEDIMENTS

The prohibitions established by blood kinship (nasab) are as follows:

-- female ascendants, e.g., mother, mother's mother, father's mother, etc.

-- female lineal descendants

-- offspring of one's parents, e.g. full of half sisters of the mother's or father's side and their offspring, and female offspring of one's brothers.

-- offspring of one's male and female grandparents, if the former are one degree removed, e.g. paternal and maternal aunts. Both their children and the children of paternal and maternal uncles of whatever degree are permitted.

In the case of kinship by marriage, the prohibition is determined by the existence of marriage (regardless of whether it has been consummated) between a man and one of his prospective wife's relatives or between a woman and one of her prospective husband's relatives. Those women prohibited are:

-- the wife's female ascendants of all degrees;

-- the wives of a man's male ascendants of whatever degree.

-- the wives of one's offspring, of whatever degree.

A woman is not permitted to marry a former husband's brother or any of his male ancestors.

The concept of a legally binding milk relationship is uniquely Islamic. A legal relationship is established between the infant who is suckled by a wet nurse and both the woman who gives such and her husband. Muslim jurists hold that because the infant takes nourishment from the body of the wet nurse, its body becomes part of hers, just as it is part of the body of the woman who nourished it in her womb. Thus, any woman who suckles an infant becomes, for legal purposes, a mother of the child. Similarly, her husband is considered a father of the child because he was responsible for the pregnancy that created the milk. The relatives of both the milk mother and the milk father are related to the child to the same degree that the would be if the milk parents were the actual parents. A Muslim is forbidden to marry persons in various categories of suckling kin.

TEMPORARILY IMPEDIMENTS

Certain relationships and conditions act as temporary bars to marriage. It is not permissible to conclude a marriage contract with the wife of another man or with a woman who is in idda, a waiting period following the death of, or her divorce from, her husband. The length of the <u>idda</u> is about three months for a divorced woman and four months and ten days for a woman whose husband has died. The idda period is to endure that the woman is not carrying a child from her previous relationship. When the idda period has passed, the woman may remarry because the relationship that caused the prohibition, i.e., the claim of her former husband, has ended.

The conclusion of a marriage contract with a person who does not follow one of the revealed religions (i.e., Judaism, Christianity, and Islam) is not valid. In addition, a Muslim woman may not marry any man unless he accepts Islam, because the relation of the children is that of the father. The reason for the stipulation is that the customs of Islam are close to the spirit of the other revealed religions, but far removed from paganism. It is therefore possible for a Muslim husband and his Christian or Jewish wife to live together in harmony, each following his/her religion.

A woman who has been divorced three times by the same husband is prohibited to him until she has been married to another (see below, "Divorce"). Remarriage after a marriage to another man is permitted because it is possible that the man may have improved his conduct by long absence from her or that the woman may have improved her conduct by association with another man.

Simultaneous marriage to two wives who are closely related, <u>viz.</u>, sisters or aunt and her niece, is not permitted, because being married to the same man could give rise to hostility between them.

A Muslim man who has four wives - - the maximum permitted at any one time – cannot contract a valid marriage with a fifth woman until he has separated from one of the four and her period of <u>idda</u> has passed.

FREEDOM OF CHOICE

An adult and mentally sound male has freedom of choice regarding marriage. Most Muslim jurists consider the age of adulthood to be 15 years, but in various countries this age is increased if requisite financial and other conditions are not met.

Most of the jurists agree that nobody can force an adult and mentally sound woman into a marriage without her consent. The only dissent in this point comes from the classical jurists al-Shafii, who allows the forcing of a virgin into marriage. Jurists have held, however, that the woman alone should not make the choice, but should be assisted in this by a relative who is her guardian, if she has no guardian she can ask the <u>qadi</u> (Muslim judge) for permission to marry. Also, if she has a guardian and disagrees with him on the subject, she takes her case to the <u>qadi.</u>

Several states have acted to limit child marriages. In India, a Muslim bride must be over the age of 14 and the groom over 18. In Pakistan, a bride must be over 16 and she can (up until the age of 18) repudiate a marriage arranged for her before her 16th birthday. In Egypt, where registration is required for a marriage to be recognized by the state, registration is prohibited for any union in which the parties have not reached the ages of 16 (females) and 18 (males).

According to the Abu Hanifa school, a woman has complete freedom to choose her husband and conclude a marriage contract herself. No one can force her to accept her guardian as an associate

201

as long as she is of age, of sound mind, and makes a suitable choice (described below). Several Islamic countries accept Abu Hanifa's idea of freedom of marital choice. These countries include: Egypt, the Sudan, Syria, Lebanon, Iraq and Pakistan; is also followed by Muslims of India, China, and Japan.

Hanafi jurists are as strict regarding the conditions of suitability (kifaa) for the couple as they are liberal in granting freedom to a woman to choose her husband. All other jurists are less exacting in the former respect. The Malikites, for instance, judge suitability only on the grounds of religious affiliation, piety, and freedom of the man from bodily defects. For the Hanafis, six conditions determine suitability: Lineage, Islam, free status, financial suitability, similarity in rectitude and piety, and occupation. Any great disparity in the bride's condition from that of the groom's in these conditions establishes unsuitability.

This stress on suitability stems from the consideration of marriage as a relationship between two families; there must be the greatest possible degree of agreement between them. Custom (urf) does not prohibit a woman of low status from marrying a man of noble origin, because it raises her position. But a woman of noble origin does not improve the low status of her husband.

PROVISION OF THE MARRIAGE CONTRACT

Neither contracting party can make provisions in the marriage contract that contradict Islamic marriage laws but some legal schools hold that additional stipulations are permissible and enforceable. For example, the Hanbali school, which is followed in Saudi Arabia and Qatar, permits a woman to stipulate that her husband will not take her on his travels or marry any other woman while he is married to her. In all schools a woman can make the condition that surety must be provided for expenditures for the bride-price. Such a condition is always valid because it confirms conditions that already exist.

The law does not impose any financial duty on a wife with respect to marital life. There are no expenditures or dowry that she must meet, and her husband has no authority over her property. Indeed, she has full freedom to manage her property, which is independent of his. Marriage restricts the financial freedom only to a small degree and that only in one school. The Malikites say that if a woman is married, she cannot give away more than one-third of her property; otherwise she is free to do what she likes with her property.

The most important legal right that marriage creates between the spouses is that of mutual inheritance (tawarruth) (see below, "Inheritance"). The other rights are: bride-price, support, and obedience.

THE BRIDE-PRICE (MAHR)

The bride-price is money the husband must pay to the wife in accordance with the marriage contract, but it is not a requisite for a valid contract. The mahr must be on a par with that received by other women of equal status in the bride's family. There is no upper limit to the bride-price, but whatever sum is mentioned in the contract must be paid.

The entire bride-price need not be paid at the time the contact is concluded. It may be deferred either in whole or in part, depending on the agreement. In some Muslim countries, a tendency has developed to reduce the sum paid at the conclusion of the contract and to increase the amount that is deferred. The deferred amount must be paid in full upon the termination of the contract, i.e., divorce or death of one of the spouses. The deferred mahr thus acts as a kind of alimony decided in advance. Thus, if a man wishes to divorce his wife he must fulfill the mahr before the divorce can be concluded. In the event of the husband's death, the wife receives her mahr from his estate above and beyond the inheritance due her. If the wife dies before she has received the mahr, it is paid to her family.

The bride-price is not rigidly fixed because of the contract. It is confirmed in toto upon the consummation of the marriage and upon the death of one of the spouses. However, the mahr is reduced by half if a husband separates from her, if the causes of separation lie on his side. All of the bride-price is cancelled if the wife, for reasons of her own, separates herself from her husband before the marriage has been consummated.

The schools of law differ on what constitutes consummation. Only the Shafiis hold that sexual intercourse alone constitutes consummation. The Hanabalis consider kissing and embracing to be sufficient. And the Malikites and Hanafis consider the seclusion of the couple in a place where they cannot be observed to constitute consummation.

The requirement of the bride-price is in the nature of a gift, for which reason the Qur'an calls it a nihla or hadiyya. This gift is required of the man, but not the woman, because it is essentially the man who does the working and earning in life; a woman's working for gain remains exceptional in many Islamic countries. When the woman comes to her husband she needs clothing,

204

jewelry, and other things appropriate to her wedded life. It therefore is the man's duty to aid her in this from his financial resources.

Because there are no legal upper limits on the amount of the mahr, its price has risen dramatically in some areas, particularly in the oil-exporting countries of the Arabian Peninsula. The Ulema (religious leaders) of Saudi Arabia have issued a series of statements entreating families to consider smaller mahrs, in the interest of society. Mahrs in excess of $50,000 have become common there, which has led to postponement of marriage and consequently a higher average marriage age for Saudi males. In such a sexually segregated society, this creates significant discontent.

SUPPORT (NAFAQA)

It is the husband's duty to support his wife as soon as she moves into his house, or prepares to do so. If he asks her to move and she refuses, she has no claim to being supported by him unless her refusal is for a legal cause, such as:

- - the husband has failed to make the required advance on the bride-price

- - the house is not up to that prescribed by law as fitting to one of her status; or

- - the house is inhabited by his family and it would not be to her advantage to live with them.

The majority of Muslim jurists concur that the wife should be supported in a style that is in conformity with the husband's status. In the event that the husband refuses to support his wife, the Hanafi school permits his imprisonment until he does. The majority of jurists hold that she can request a separation on the grounds of such refusal and that the qadi can grant her a divorce if such grounds are established.

If the husband has fallen into financial difficulties and is unable to support his wife, the Hanafi school does not release him from the obligation to support her, but provides that she should be supported by one of her relatives. Such support becomes a claim against the husband, the payment of which can be demanded if his financial condition improves. The majority of jurists permit a wife to request a separation in the case of a husband's inability to support her.

OBEDIENCE

An obedient wife is a husband's right. By obedience is meant that the wife should transfer to the husband's domicile and that they should live together in harmony. She can refuse to move to his domicile only for the reasons already stated.

MIXED MARRIAGES

With few exceptions, a Christian or a Jew marries a Muslim and resides in an Islamic country will be subject to those provisions of Islamic family law obtaining in that country. A Muslim man may contract a valid marriage to a Christian or Jewish woman and she is under no compulsion to convert to Islam. In these circumstances:

-- Any children born to her will be considered Muslim. The will usually also be considered citizens of the father's country.

-- The husband's permission is always needed for the children to leave an Islamic country despite the fact that the children will also have, for example, American citizenship. Foreign immigration authorities can be expected to enforce these regulations. The ability of U.S. consular officers to aid an American woman who wishes to leave the country with her children is very limited.

-- Although she will have recourse to the courts, she may be divorced by her husband with little difficulty. If there is no-premarital contract as is customary in Islamic countries (see above, "The Bride-Price"), she may find herself without alimony.

-- She may initiate divorce, but the grounds for such an action are more limited than in the West.

-- Although she will be entitled to child support for a period which varies somewhat from state to state, at a certain point of age the children will come under the custody of the father or his family (see below "Guardianship and Support")

-- With the exception of Tunisia, Turkey, and South Yemen, her husband may contract (or in Iraq the petition the court for permission to contract) an additional marriage or marriages unless it is stipulated in their marriage contract that he cannot without her permission.

-- In most Islamic countries, if she remains non-Muslim, she cannot inherit from her husband nor can he inherit from her.

-- In Islamic countries she will need the permission of her husband to leave the country.

A Christian or Jewish man may marry a Muslim woman in an Islamic country provided that he first converts to Islam. Whatever his citizenship, he then becomes subject to Islamic family law if he resides in the country. He would thus be legally responsible for the financial commitment to his wife specified earlier ("The Bride-Price" and "Support").

POLYGAMY

In Islamic states except Tunisia, South Yemen, and Turkey, where polygamy is expressly prohibited, a Muslim man may take up to four wives, provided he has the financial capability and the personal disposition to treat them equally. Polygamous unions are now becoming a rarity, in part because of the rising expense of marriage but predominantly because of the social disapproval expressed toward polygamy in the majority of Muslim countries.

In many Islamic countries, although a man may marry several women, there are legal inhibitions which prevent him from doing so with ease. A few examples follow:

-- In Iraq, a man must have permission from a qadi (judge). To acquire this, he must demonstrate financial competency and prove that some benefit will accrue to the family unit as a whole.

-- In Morocco, the first wife may initiate court action to block additional marriages.

208

- - In Pakistan, a man must appeal to an arbitration council to which the first wife names a represĕntative.

DIVORCE (TALAQ)

From the Islamic viewpoint, any marriage contract (including non-Islamic ones) automatically terminates when anything occurs that makes continuation of the marriage incompatible with Islamic precepts. Examples of these special circumstances include:

- - apostasy from Islam by either partner;

- - a conversion to Islam by the wife where the husband is non-Muslim; or

- - the conversion to Islam by either partner of a pagan couple.

(Muslim women in India before the enactment of the reform laws occasionally resorted to apostasy to dissolve their marriages if their husbands and the religious courts were unresponsive.)

If a woman wants a divorce, she normally must apply to a qadi. This reflects the fact that the husband undertook financial responsibilities with regard to the marriage; made an advance payment on the bride-price and is to pay the balance upon divorce; and has furnished the house, incurring many expenses. If the wife could divorce him on her own responsibility, he would lose all that he had spent on her.

The qadi's involvement is designed to ascertain that she is requesting a divorce because she has been wronged. If such is the case, then the husband bears the consequences and loses his financial investment in her. If it is established that the husband is

209

the wronged party, then the qadi divorces them on condition that the wife reimburse the husband.

A wife can divorce herself from her husband without the intervention of a qadi only if, when the contract is drawn up, a condition to that effect is made, accompanied by a tafwid (authorization) giving the wife the right to divorce herself whenever she chooses. This right can also be granted by a husband to a wife in the course of a marriage.

Because a man can divorce a procedure to ensure that it cannot be concluded in the heat of the moment. Divorce exists in three degrees:

- - Revocable divorce (al-talaq al raji) means that the husband can take his wife back during the period of idda (waiting period). This divorce is charged against his account as a caution against his divorcing her a second time. If the idda passes without his taking her back, the divorce becomes one of the second degree.

- - The second degree (al-talaq al-bain baynunatun sughra) applies when the first degree is fulfilled or if the couple has not had intercourse. In this divorce, the two parties can resume married life only by concluding a new contract and the husband's paying of another mahr (bride-price).

- - The third category (al bain naynunatun kubra) is a divorce fulfilled by three repudiations. In this case the husband can marry the wife again only after she lived as a wife with another man under a valid contract.

In all schools a woman may petition a qadi for divorce. A divorce granted by the qadi at the request of the woman belongs, according to the Malikites, to the first category; that is, it can be revoked if it is granted for non-support and support is reinstituted. The Shafiites and Hanbalis hold that such a divorce belongs to the second category (i.e., that it is irrevocable) if:

-- it is due to a deep-seated and longstanding or permanent defects in the husband and if the woman cannot live with him without injury, e.g., if he is insane or suffering from elephantiasis, leprosy, or impotence;

-- if it is because of injury done by the husband to the wife, such as treating her in a way not proper to her status or remaining absent from her for a year or more, even if he leaves her enough money for her expenses. In such a case, if she seeks a divorce and the qadi grants it, it is a clear divorce (talaq bain).

Hanafi law is quite strict compared with other schools. It acknowledges only two grounds for divorce: the husband's impotence, and the exercise of the option of puberty (where a contract was arranged for a minor female by her guardian). In Pakistan where the Hanafi school predominates, reformers drew on Malikite law to supplement the limited Hanafi grounds for divorce initiated by the wife. Thus they added desertion, failure to maintain, imprisonment for seven years or more, failure to perform marital obligations, severe or chronic (mental or physical) defects, and cruelty and maltreatment. In 1955, incompatibility was added to the acceptable grounds for divorce, based on Qur'anic verse. Egypt has drawn on Malikite law in the same way.

211

Pakistani law also provides that a man give notice of intention to divorce to the chairman (appointed by the governor) of a family law arbitration council. The divorce does not become legally binding for 90 days after notice has been given. Within 30 days, however, the chairman must appoint an arbitration council which endeavors to reconcile the couple.

In Tunisia, there is no divorce outside the court system. Mutual consent between spouses is sufficient grounds for divorce in addition to a wide variety of other grounds. An indemnity may be paid to either husband or wife, depending upon the financial resources of each.

CHILDREN'S RIGHT

Birth control is permitted by Islam as long as it does not injure the mother or is not accomplished by coitus interruptus, which is considered injurious to health. Abortion is prohibited except in cases where the mother's life is gravely endangered. The child's rights are fixed from the time of birth. Some of these are related to the father, some to both parents, and some to the mother. The first right is the establishment of the child's paternity, followed by food, upbringing, care for the child and its possessions, and support.

ESTBALISHMENT OF KINSHIP

Provisions governing the establishment of paternity are based on four principles:

- - A valid marriage contract establishes a child's paternity. The Hanafis do not even make it a condition that the spouses must have had an opportunity to have sexual intercourse after the

212

marriage, while the Hanbalis, Malikites, and Shafiis assert that sexual intercourse at least must have been possible.

- - The minimum time for a child to be born alive after a marriage so that it may inherit, be inherited from, and be possessed of rights is six lunar months. If a woman bears a living child less than six months after her marriage, her husband may nevertheless, claim it as his own. Jurists differ on the maximum period of pregnancy, varying from five years to nine months, with one year being the median. In the case of a child born to a woman in idda, the child's paternity can be denied only if the woman gives birth more than one year after the death or her divorce from her husband.

- - If a married woman commits adultery, the paternity of her child is attributed to her husband unless he repudiates it.

- - Acknowledgement by the husband fixes paternity.

SUCKLING

Suckling is a right due to the infant from its mother and father. It is the mother's duty to suckle and the father's to provide for the mother's support. If the mother refuses to suckle, the law does not compel her unless: the child will take no breast but hers; no one else can be found to suckle; or the child and the father are so poor that they cannot pay anyone else, and there is no one to donate the money. The father under any circumstances can give the child out to a wet nurse. The cost suckling a child may be taken from the infant's property, if it possesses any, or is to be born by the father or the father's family.

GUARDIANSHIP AND SUPPORT

There are three types of guardianship (wilaya), which are fixed for a child from the time of its birth;

- - The first is guardianship of upbringing (tarbiya), which is overseen by women. In the absence of the mother, this devolves upon the mother's family, although expenses are borne by the father or are paid from the child's property. The age at which this period of dependence terminates varies: some schools fix it at 7 years for a son and 9 for a daughter, others at 9 and 11, respectively. Certain jurists have not set an age limit but have left it at the age when the child can do without women's help, dress and feed itself, and look after its household affairs. In the case of divorced parents, it is permissible for a daughter to remain with her mother if the parents agree. But such an agreement cannot be made for a son, who, after the age of dependence, "needs to learn what is customary for men to know,"

- - The second is the child's spiritual guardianship. The spiritual guardian may be the father or a full-blooded male relative of the father. This period lasts until puberty for a male child, unless he is not considered to be responsible by that time. The age of puberty is generally considered to be 15 lunar years for both boys and girls. A female child remains under the guardian as long as she remains a virgin, unless she remains unmarried past the customary age or acquires sufficient understanding to mange her own affairs. When she marries, the spiritual guardianship over ceases.

- - The third is guardianship over child's property which usually is carried out by the father or his appointee, the paternal grandfather, or a qadi. This period also usually concludes at puberty if the child gives evidence of maturity and financial sense. Several countries such as Egypt have deemed it advisable that the termination of the property trusteeship take place when the child has reached 21 solar years of age. There is no difference between a girl and a boy as far as property guardianship is concerned.

In all cases, a minor is to be supported by his or her own property, if any, or secondly by the father or the father's family. In no case does the child's mother, even if she is wealthy, have to provide for the material support of the child inasmuch as, in Islam, marriage is not a financial partnership between the spouses.

FINANCIAL ORGANIZATION OF THE FAMILY

Islam creates property relationships that make the family a cooperative economic and social unit. Three major areas of mutual financial assistance are incumbent on the family.

- - If a family member commits a crime expiable by an appropriate financial penalty, the latter is to be paid by the blood-related members of the family (aqila). These are a person's relatives who belong to the same clan (asaba), i.e., the relatives on the paternal side. The initial responsibility falls upon the one who stands closest in line of inheritance.

- - The duty of supporting a poor relative falls upon a wealthy relative, no matter what the degree of relationship, although the closest relative has priority.

215

-- Inheritance devolves upon all relatives, although priority goes to those who are closest in degree and strength of relationship.

INHERITANCE

For Muslims, testate and intestate succession lies at the heart of Islamic law. This is because the precise fractional shares in an estate to which a variety of relatives are entitles are prescribed in the Qur'an. They are technically called <u>faraid</u>, a plural of <u>fard</u>, used for a duty imposed by divine command.

Inheritance is the most complex of all Islamic family laws, as can be seen from the classical model that follows. Many Islamic countries have enacted inheritance law reforms, some of them as complicated as the classical model. Egypt, Iraq, Sudan, Tunisia, Lebanon, Syria, and Morocco all have enacted reforms that basically strengthen the claims of the nuclear family, especially wives and daughters, to the detriment of agnatic heirs (see "Definition of Terms.").

As set forth in the Qur'an there are two categories of heirs: the sharers, also called Qur'anic heirs, and the residuaries.

The sharers are:

(1.) The husband
(2.) The wife
(3.) The daughter
(4.) the daughter of a son however far removed in descendance
(5.) the father
(6.) the mother
(7.) the true grandfather, however far removed

(8.)   the true grandmother, however far removed
(9.)   the full sister
(10.) the consanguine sister
(11.) the uterine brother
(12.) the uterine sister

DEFINITION OF TERMS:

true grandfather: an ascendant between whom and the descendant no female is interposed.

true grandmother: an ascendant between whom and the descendant no male ancestor is interposed who is separated from the descendant by a female. Thus the father's mother and the mother's mother are true grandmothers; the mother's father's mother's is not.

consanguine sister: a half sister related to the descendant through the father.

uterine brother/sister: a half brother or sister related to the descendant through the mother.

daughter of a son: includes a son's daughter, a son's son's daughter, etc., however far removed.

The shares of various sharers are as follows:

(1.)   **husband**   1/4; if there is a child or a son's child no matter how far removed; 1/2 if there is no such child.

217

(2.) **wife**   1/8; if there are several wives they take 1/8 collectively, to be divided equally among them. 1/8 is received if there is a child or a son's child no matter how far removed; if there is no such child the share is 1/4

(3.) **daughter**   1/2; several daughters take 2/3 collectively. These shares apply if there is no son. If there is a son, daughters take as residuaries.

(4.) **The daughter of a son, no matter how far removed**
1/2; 2/3 if there are several daughters in this category taking collectively. These shares apply if there is no son or daughter, no higher son's son, no higher son's daughter, or no equal son's son. If there is a son or a higher son's son, or if there are several daughters or a higher son's daughters, the daughter of a son does not take anything; she is excluded from the inheritance. If, however, there is only one daughter or a higher son's daughter, the daughter or higher son's daughter will take 1/2; the daughter of a son dealt with here will take 1/6. If the daughter of a son competes with an equal son's son, she becomes a residuary.

(5.) **father**   1/6 if there is a child or a child of a son however far removed, or two or more brothers or sisters of the decedent, whether such brothers or sisters are full, consanguine or uterine. If there is no child or a son's child however far removed or not more than one brother or sister, the mother takes 1/3. However, although collaterals may restrict the mother to 1/6, they will not inherit if the decedent's father survives. If a wife or husband of the decedent survives together with the decedent's father, the mother takes 1/3 of what remains after the share of the wife or husband has been deducted.

(6.)   **mother**   1/6 if there is a child or a child of a son however far removed, or two or more brothers or sister's of the decedent, whether such brothers or sisters are full, consanguine or uterine. If there is no child or a son's child however far removed or not more than one brother or sister, the mother takes 1/3. However, although collaterals may restrict the mother to 1/6, they will not inherit if the decedent's father survives. If a wife or husband of the decedent survives together with the decedent's father, the mother takes 1/3 of what remains after the share of the wife or husband has been deducted.

(7.)   **grandfather (however far removed)**
1/6; he is entirely excluded by the father of the decedent of a nearer true grandfather. Otherwise, his position is the same as the father's would be were he living.

(8.) **grandmother (however far removed)**

1/6; whether there is one or several. The maternal grandmother is entirely excluded by the mother or a nearer maternal or paternal grandmother. The paternal grandmother is entirely excluded by the mother, the father, a true grandfather, or a nearer true maternal or paternal grand mother.

(9.) **full sister**

1/2; if there is one; 2/3 collectively if there are several. A full sister is entirely excluded by a son, a son's son however, far removed), the father, or the true grandfather. If there is a full brother, the full sister becomes a residuary.

(10.) **consanguine sister**

1/2; if there is one; 2/3 collectively if there are several. A consanguine sister is entirely excluded by a son, a son's son however far removed), the father, or a true grandfather, as well as a full brother or more that one full sister. If there is only one full sister, the consanguine sister becomes a residuary with a consanguine brother.

(11.) **uterine brother**

1/6; if there is one; 2/3 collectively if there are several. A consanguine sister is entirely

220

excluded by a son, a son's son (however far removed), the father, or a true grandfather.

(12.) uterine sister

Same as uterine brother.

An agnate is person who is related to the decedent through male links only. This would include such persons as the son and the son's son, but also the son's daughter; the father, the father's father, and so forth. Residuaries can be divided into descendants, ascendants, and collateral relatives; among the latter are included not only brothers and sisters of the decedent, but also the paternal uncle both full and consanguine, and his son remoter descendants. Among the male agnates, the son takes only as a residuary; that is assuming there is only one son, he will take what is left after the shares of the Qur'anic heirs have been satisfied.

ENFORCEABILITY AND THE FUTURE OF ISLAMIC LAW

Because Islamic law and religious morality are often inextricably merged into a general philosophy of life, there is for Muslims a positive coercion towards certain observances that lack civil sanctions. Additionally, from the strictly spiritual point of view, Islamic law must be observed by a Muslim even in the absence of a civil authority to enforce it. A Muslim who does not act in consonance with Islamic law at the very least imperils his spiritual salvation.

In the Quran, the primary material source of Sharia, there is no clear or consistent distinction between the moral and the legal rule. This led Islamic courts traditionally to maintain a distinction

221

between the rule that is legally enforceable and that which is morally desirable.

Recent developments in family law, however, have produced a synthesis of law and morality. Standards of behavior regarded by the traditional authorities as imposing a moral obligation have now been transformed into the legal requirements. The effect of the majority of the legislation has been to ensure a greater measure or rights, particularly for women and children.

In the realm of contemporary family law, Islam is witnessing a resurgence of legal moralism. The courts applying Islamic law today, in deciding whether a divorce is for "just cause," whether a proposed polygamous union is without prejudice to the wife's right of equal treatment, or whether to make a bequest on behalf of a deceased who failed in his personal duty to do so, are enforcing ethical standards that are at the root of Sharia doctrine, but which have been ignored by the practice of Sharia courts. As a result, easy divorce and polygamy are becoming more infrequent, and a man's marital responsibilities more sharply defined.

16960/WP+53 5/91

ADDENDUM

The following is a list of certificates that can be used for marriage by the Imam. These are:

A. Certificate and Declaration of Islamic Faith
B. Pre-Marriage Agreement
C. Certificate of Marriage (Nikah)
D. Certificate of Divorce (Khul'ah)

These are only a sample and a guide for the Imam who is involved in officiating a marriage. We wish happiness to all.

I seek refuge in Allah from the outcast Shaitan. In the name of Allah, the Most Gracious, the Most Merciful. O Allah! You are the Opener of the doors of blessings, please open for us the best door of blessings.

CERTIFICATE AND DECLARATION
OF ISLAMIC FAITH

This is to certify that:_____
has accepted the Faith of Islam on this_____
day of _____ in the year_____
willingly by declaring the shahadah as follows:

(1)   **Ash-Hadu Ann La Ilaha Illa Allah.**
      *(I bear witness that there is no one worthy of worship
      except the Only One God (Allah).*

(2)   **Wa Ash-Hadu Anna Muhammadan Abduhu wa
      Rasuluh.**
      *(And I bear witness that Muhammad is the servant
      and the final prophet and messenger of Allah.)*

This declaration has been made before me and the following
witnesses:

Signature:_____

Officiating Imam/Religious Supervisor:_____

Witness (1): _____

Witness (2): _____

Date of Issue: _____

Nationality: _____

Previous Faith: _____

Previous Name: _____

Muslim Name:_____

PRE-MARRIAGE AGREEMENT

We, the undersigned, (Groom) _____and
(Bride) _____ agree on this day
_____ to the following terms between
us, so that our marriage will last forever with happiness.

1. We marry in the name of Allah, the Creator of the Universe.

2. Our marriage shall be according to the Islamic Law (Shari'ah).

3. Our divorce (if it takes place) shall be according to Islamic Law.

4. Our children shall be raised as Muslims.

5. Our living habits (inside and outside the house) shall be according to the teachings of Islam.

6. The custody of the children shall be according to the Islamic teachings.

7. The inheritance shall be according to the Islamic Jurisprudence.

8. The rites of burial shall be according to the Islamic rituals.

9. If and when a problem would be created between us and/or with others, we shall go to a Muslim community and religious leader, a Qadi (Judge), a Mufti, an `Alim, and/or or a Muslim Council of Qada' (Jurisprudence), a Muslim Council of Arbitration/Reconciliation.

10. If by any chance, a non-Muslim Judge or a non-Muslim lawyer is to handle any case of our affairs, they should rule our case(s) according to the teachings of Islam, i.e., they should seek the help, advice and opinion of a Muslim religious leader so as they execute and enforce the teachings of Islam upon us.

We, the undersigned, pray to Almighty Allah to help us to honor this agreement. We take Allah, the Creator of the Universe, as our witness. A promissory note (for mahr) is attached to this agreement. We make this pledge and this agreement in front of the following witnesses:

Groom: _____   _____
              (print name)   Signature

Bride: _____   _____
              (print name)   Signature

Witness(1):_____   _____
                    (print name)   Signature

Witness(2):_____   _____
                    (print name)   Signature

Date of this contract:_____

Overseeing this contract:_____

226

CERTIFICATE OF MARRIAGE
(Nikah)

On this day of_____14_____A.H. _____
19_____ CE., I, _____
representative of _____, have
officiated the marriage ceremony of the following couple
in accordance with the Islamic Shari'ah (law).

GROOM:

I,_____ , solemnly propose to marry
Miss _____ , and take her as my wife.
I agree to pay as a Mahr to her now in the sum of   US
$ _____, and a later Mahr in the amount of US
$_____.

BRIDE:

I, _____, accept your
solemn
proposal to take me as your wife. I accept an early Mahr
of US$ _____ and a later Mahr of US$ _____

DECLARATIONS

1. We make this declaration before the present witnesses, praying to Almighty Allah to be our witness. Allah is the Best of all Witnesses.

2. We also declare here that while our marriage is according to the Islamic Law, our divorce, if it should take place, will also be according to the Islamic Law.

3. We wish to declare here that our children will be raised Muslims.

Groom _____   Address_____
           (Signature)   _____

Bride_____   Address_____
           (Signature)   _____

Wakeel (Lawful)_____   Address_____
           (Signature)   _____

Witness(1)_____   Address_____
           (Signature)   _____

Witness(2)_____   Address_____
           (Signature)   _____

Officiated By:_____
           (Representative)

Date:_____

CERTIFICATE OF DIVORCE (KHUL'AH)

I,_____, representative of _____, have met the following individuals and witnesses on this day _____ A.H. and _____ A.D. at _____ AM/PM. Ms._____ with Mr. _____ (father), uncle, guardian, wakeel), and Mr./Ms. _____ _____ as her witnesses in the City of _____, State of _____. I listened to her problems involving her husband, Mr. _____. Her story was witnesed by the witnesses. Documents of her marriage certificate from _____ were presented as well as documents of her divorce from the Court of ____ _____ issued on _____in the City of _____, State of _____.

Her case is summarized as follows:

(1)   Her husband deserted her in _____.
(2)   She could not locate his presence in USA.
        Yes _____ No _____

229

(3) She was granted divorce from the Court in USA.
     Yes _____ No _____

(4) Her waiting period for desertion (minimum six months) is met.
     Yes _____ No _____

(5) She is asking for Khul'ah (Divorce) with her full consent without being pressured by anyone.
     Yes _____ No _____

(6) Her request was agreed upon by the witnesses.
     Yes _____ No _____

Therefore, I shall testify that her Khul'ah be granted to her as of _____.This Khul'ah is granted with the condition that Ms. _____ is to have three more menstruating waiting period before she has the right to remarry another Muslim man.

OFFICATED BY: _____

Date: _____

Witness (1) _____

Witness (2) _____

Signature of the lady:_____

A Course on

Islamic Shari'ah
Topic: Family

EXAMS

The following is a series of questions I, II, III, IV, and V regarding Family in Islam. They are very helpful and provocative to the general reader. It was thought that the reader will enjoy answering them independently; and then sharing them with his/her family members and later with his/her friends.

The answers are included after each exam. Try to answer them without seeing the answers; then look for the answers and compare. If you disagree with any of them, please write directly to the author.

231

EXAM # I   MATCHING QUESTIONS

Match column B with Column A. there is only one item in B
to match with Column A. Select the right word in Column B
and write the letter of that word in Column A.

1. Hijab	_____	A.	Woman divorcing her husband
2. Hadanah	_____	B.	Adultery
3. Laqeetah	_____	C.	Abortion
4. Qurba	_____	D.	Reception after child deliver
5. Khul'ah	_____	E.	Man divorcing his wife
6. Takafful	_____	F.	Orphan
7. Zina	_____	G.	Custody
8. Asheera	_____	H.	Nisa' (women)
9. Nikah	_____	I.	Adoption
10. Ijhaad	_____	J.	Shura
11. Waleemah	_____	K.	Illegitimate child
12. Irth	_____	L.	Khitbah
13. Aqeeqah	_____	M.	Khimar
14. Yateem	_____	N.	Fostering
15. Tabanni	_____	O.	Kins and Kiths
		P.	Zawj
		Q.	Marriage
		R.	Inheritance
		S.	Reception after Marriage
		T.	Tribe

Answers to Exam # 1   1. M 2. G 3. K 4. O 5. A 6. N 7. B 8. T 9. Q 10. C 11. S
12. R 13. D 14. F 15. I

232

1. The meaning of the word Zawaj is:

   a. Husband   b. Wife
   c. Pairs   d. Marriage
   e. All of the above

2. The meaning of the word Talaq is:

   a. Marriage   b. Nikah
   c. Aqeeqah   d. Kitbah
   e. None of the above

3. The meaning of the word Tabanni is:

   a. Waleemah   b. Nikah
   c. Hadanah   d. Yateem
   e. Adoption

4. The word Takafful means:

   a. Custody   b. Adoption
   c. Abortion   d. Fostering
   e. Hadanah

5. The word Hadanah is to mean:

   a. Tabanni   b. Takafful
   c. Mawaddah   d. Shura
   e. Custody

6. The meaning of the word Ijhaad is:

a. Tabanni   b. Hijab
c. Khitbah   d. Nikah
e. Abortion

7. The closest meaning for the word Laqeetah is:

a. Aqeeqah   b. Zina
c. Lost/Found child   d. Sifah
e. Yateem

8. Hijab may mean:

a. Nikah   b. Sifah
c. Nisa'   d. Khimar
e. None of the above

9. Waleemah is a general terminology used to mean:

a. Aqeeqah   b. Zawaj
c. Nikah   d. Sifah
e. Reception after marriage

10. The plural of the word Imra'ah is:

a. Rijal   b. Asheera
c. Zawjah/Azwaj   d. Nisa'
e. Family

Answers to Exam # II
1. d 2. e 3. e 4. d 5. e 6. e 7. c 8. d 9. e 10. d

EXAM III TRUE OR FALSE QUESTIONS

1. _____In Islam there should not be a pre marriage agreement between groom and bride.

2. _____ If pre marriage agreement has to be made between groom and bride, it is the right of the husband to see his rights. The bride has to accept whatever the groom stipulates.

3. _____ While it is Halal to perform marriage according to Shari'ah of Islam, it is Haram to perform the secular marriage along with the religious one at the same time by the same Imam.

4._____ If a person marries a non-Muslim (Ahli-Khitab) girl it is Halal for him to perform the marriage by a priest/ minister in a church just to please her parents, community and her religious teachings.

5._____If a woman wishes to take Khul'ah from her husband, she is not to receive her benefits from her husband including the custody of the children.

6._____ If a divorce takes place between husband and wife due to the initiation of the husband, he is entitled to the children as long as they are under the age of puberty.

7._____When a Muslim man marries a Christian woman, she is entitled to stay as a Christian and the children are entitled to become Christians.

8._____A non-Muslim wife is entitled to inherit her husband

9._____A non-Muslim wife with children from a previous marriage are also entitled to inherit the step-father after his death.

10._____Parents of a deceased person have no right to inherit their son after his death.

Bonus Points

1._____ Brothers and sisters are to inherit their deceased brother even if he has children who are minors.

2._____ It is totally Haram to benefit from the wealth of orphans especially while you are fostering them, and even if you are in need of financial help.

3._____ After death, it is Halal to cremate a Muslim if he has already written in his will to do so.

4._____ After death, it is Halal to cremate a Muslim if he has already written in his will to do so.

5._____It is O.K. for a man to divorce his wife, but she has no legal right to divorce her husband.

Answers to Exam III

        1. F 2. F 3. F 4. F 5. F 6. F 7. F 8. F 9. F
        10. F

Bonus

1. F 2. F 3. F 4. F 5. F

EXAM IV   TRUE OR FALSE QUESTIONS

1. _____ When a problem starts between husband and wife, either one should call the police immediately.

2._____ When a problem takes place in a family, both, the husband and wife should go immediately to see a psychiatrist.

3._____When a problem is created between husband and wife, each one should remind the other party about his/her bad habits and previous silly mistakes so that he/she will cool down.

4._____When husband and wife get into an argument, they should swear at each other so that each one will cool down.

5._____When a problem starts in a family, the wife should immediately call her relatives to get involved in their private affairs.

6. _____ If and when a husband says something wrong, the wife should never ever keep silent. She should immediately correct him.

7. _____ Husband and wife should discuss their problems in front of their children, so that they will learn in advance.

8. _____ A husband should check regularly on his wife as to whom she talks to on the phone. The best way is to tap the phone.

9._____Children should bring their problems with their parents to the Weekend Islamic School to be discussed.

237

10.____ The Imam of the mosque should be informed daily about the affairs of the husband and wife in their homes, because he is the Imam.

Bonus Points

1.____ A Muslim wife has no right to spend any money of the family on anything, including Masjid, without the permission of her husband.

2.____ When a husband speaks, the wife has to listen, even if he is speaking nonsense.

3.____ The husband has the right to discipline by spanking and/or beat up his wife anytime he wishes, but the wife has no right to do so.

4.____ Islam gives preference to boys over girls, and as such the boys are to receive double inheritance.

5.____ A Muslim woman has no right to work outside her house. If she wants to work in any job, it has to be from within her house only.

Exam IV

1. F 2. F 3. F 4. F 5. F 6. F 7. F 8. F 9. F 10. F

EXAM V   TRUE OR FALSE QUESTIONS

1._____ Khitbah and Nikah are the same thing.

2._____ Waleemah and Aqeeqah are festivities for the same purpose.

3._____ Divorce and Khul'ah are the same for both Husband and Wife, without any restrictions or conditions.

4._____Polygamy, polygeny and polyender mean the same thing.

5._____Miscarriage and abortion have same causes and same procedures.

6._____ Fostering is Haram in Islam while adoption is Halal.

7._____ While Zina is Haram in Islam, premarriage sexual relationship and extramarital relationship are also Haram.

8._____In as much as a Muslim man may marry a chaste woman from Ahli-Kitab, a Muslim woman can do the same.

9._____ Hadanah and Laqeetah mean the same thing.

10._____The following items are Haram in Islam:

Abortion	Artificial Conception from any person.
Adoption	Birth control outside family
Incest	Polygamy from two sides
Rape	Mixed Swimming
Zina	Mixed Dancing
Sifah	Homosexuality

11._____The following terms are related to the Family: 'Asheerah, Arham, Qurba, ;'A-il, Ansab

12._____Family in Islam is composed of:
husband and wife and children;
Grandchildren of both husband and wife;
Parents of both husband and wife:
Brothers and sisters of both husband and wife;
Uncles of both husband and wife; and
Nephews and nieces of both husband and wife

13._____Nikah and Sifah are two words to mean the same thing.

Answers to Exam V

1. F 2. F 3. F 4. F 5. F 6. F 7. T 8. T 9. T 10. T
11. T 12. T 13. F

Allah says the truth.

Knowledge

Islam emphasizes the importance of knowledge to all mankind. It is only through true knowledge that one can appreciate the Creator of the Universe namely Allah (swt). Muslims are ordained to seek knowledge from cradle to grave and as far as a person can to obtain it.

In as much as seeking knowledge is a must on every Muslim, dissemination of knowledge is also incumbent on Muslims to the members of the society. The methods of disseminating the information should be lawful, as well as the truth is to be released to everyone. Hiding or keeping the true knowledge away from those who seek it, is considered a sin.

The best investment for every human being is through: perpetual charity (Sadaqa Jariya), useful knowledge that people shall benefit or, and a loving child who shall make special prayers for his/her parents.

LEGALITY

The Foundation has been established and registered with the Secretary of the State of Illinois since January 8,1987 as a non-profit, charitable, educational, religious and /or scientific society within the meaning of section 501 (c) (3) of the Internal Revenue Code.

The Foundation has a tax-exempt status with the IRS, and donations are considered tax-deductible.

FINANCES

The finances of the FOUNDATION are mainly from donations and contributions in the form of cash, assets and wills.

INUMERENT OF INCOME

No part of the net earnings of the Corporation shall inure to the benefit of, or be distributed to, its members, directors, officers or other private persons except that the Corporation shall be authorized and empowered to pay reasonable compensation for services rendered.

PURPOSES

The purposes of the FOUNDATION are summarized as follows:

1. To promote Islamic Knowledge through education.
2. To create a better understanding of Islam among Muslims and non-Muslims through education and communication.
3. To publish books and other literature about Islam and its teachings
4. To disseminate Islamic Knowledge and education through TV, Radio, Video, and other means of mass communications.
5. To establish ecumenical among the religious people of America so that a better understanding will be created.

ACTIVITIES

The activities of the FOUNDATION shall include, but not be limited to the following:

1. Publishing literature pertaining to Islam.
2. Producing audio cassettes and audio-visual tapes on certain topics of Islam.
3. Giving lectures related to Islam as a religion, culture and civilization.
4. Cooperation with other societies, foundations and organizations whose aims and objectives are similar to the FOUNDATION.

KNOWLEDGE IN THE QUR'AN

The word knowledge ('ILM) is mentioned in the Qur'an more than 700 times in 87 different forms. Some of the pertinent Ayat are listed below.

1. The first Ayat revealed to Prophet Muhammad (pbuh) at Cave Hira' are in Surah Al-Alaq (The Clot) (96:1-5). They are related to knowledge of embryology through scientific investigation.

2. Allah honors all those who are knowledgeable. These people cannot be compared with the ignorant ones. See Surah Al-Zumar (The Troops) (39:29)

3. Only the knowledgeable people are those who do appreciate the creations of Allah (swt) . They are the ones who respect

243

Him and worship Him with knowledge and humility. Please read Surah Fatir (The Creator) (35:28)

Knowledge is in the Hands of Allah and it is at His disposal. People are to seek the true knowledge from its source namely Allah. Read Surah Al-Mulk (The Sovereignty) (67:26).

4. People are to seek knowledge from Allah (swt) are to request Him to enrich them daily with 'ILM. Read Surah Taha (20:114).

KNOWLEDGE IN THE HADITH

Prophet Muhammad (pbuh) emphasized 'ILM tremendously and encouraged Muslims to seek knowledge in any part of the world. The following is a summary:

1. In one Hadith the Prophet says: "The Knowledgeable people ('Ulama) are the inheritors to the Prophets."

2. In another Hadith He encouraged Muslims to seek knowledge, saying: "Seeking knowledge is a must on every Muslim."

3. In another place, He demanded that knowledge is to be sought throughout lifetime, saying: "Seek knowledge from cradle to grave."

4. Knowledge is to be disseminated to all, and the best knowledge is that of the Qur'an, saying: "The best amongst you are the ones who learn Qur'an and teach it to others."

244

5. Knowledge is to be taught and to be carried on even after death. In His Hadith the Prophet said: "When a person dies, his deeds are over, except from three things; perpetual charity, a useful knowledge, or a good child who makes supplications for him."

The FOUNDATION will continue, with the help of Almighty God (Allah), to publish more useful literature.

And He (Allah) has power over all things.
(Qur'an, 11:4)

Publications

I. BOOKS ON HEALTH, FOOD AND NUTRITION:

1. Dietary Regulations & Food Habits of Muslims
2. Overeating and Behavior
3. Islam on Alcohol
4. Alcohol in Beverages, Drugs, Foods and Vitamins
5. Cheese
6. AFTO and FAO
7. Food and Overpopulation
8. Honey: Food and a Medicine
* 9. Gelatin
10. Shortening in Foods
11. A Manual on Food Shortenings
12. Food Supplementation
13. World Health Organization for Muslim Nations
* 14. A Muslim Guide to Food Ingredients
15. Natural Therapeutics of Medicine in Islam (co-authored)
16. Islamic Dietary Laws & Practices (co-authored)
17. Food and Nutrition Manual (co-authored)
18. A Handbook of Muslim Foods
* 19. Understanding Halal Foods: Fallacies and Facts
20. Pork: Possible Reasons For Its Prohibition
* 21. Book of Healing

II. BOOKS ABOUT FRIDAY KHUTAB:

* 1. Book of Al-Khutab
* 2. Islamic Orations
* 3. Orations from the Pulpit

246

IV.   PAMPHLETS:

V. Other Items

DVD's Friday Khutbah   Volume 1-3

Variety of Salat (Prayers)

*   These publications are available from:
Foundation for Islamic Knowledge

P.O. Box 665
Lombard, IL 60148
Phone: (630) 495-4817 / Fax: (630) 627-8894
e-mail: ahmadsakr@yahoo.com **website:** www.ahmadsakr.com

Allah Almighty Says The Truth

Books To Be Published

1. Arabic Expressions, Glossary, and Word Search
2. They Left ... We Follow
3. Guidance From Confusion
4. Book of Memories
5. Khutab of the Prophet
6. Khutab of Sacred Ahadith
7. Book of Khutab: Halal and Haram Foods
8. Welcome to the World of Islam
9. Al-Insaan: The Human Being
10. Speakers Bureau Guide Book
11. Islamic Perspectives
12. Islamic Understanding
13. Islam vs. Muslims
14. Health, Hygiene and Nutrition
15. Scientific Reflections from the Qur'an
16. Biological Terms in the Qur'an
17. Educational Institutions in Islam
18. Writing An Islamic Will
19. Qur'an Commentary in Summary
20. Book of Pledges
21. Selected Verses From Qur'an
22. Book Of Targheeb

These and other books will not be published unless someone like you comes forward and extend a hand of help. You may sponsor any of the above books, or any number of copies of a particular book.

Your help in any capacity is greatly needed even to pay the previous debts to the printers.

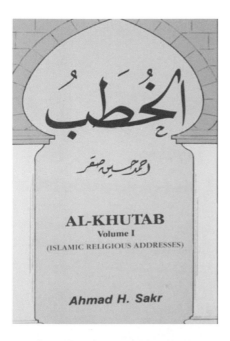

الخُطب

أحمد حسين صقر

AL-KHUTAB
Volume I
(ISLAMIC RELIGIOUS ADDRESSES)

Ahmad H. Sakr

ديوان الخُطب

Chronicle of Khutab
Volume IV

أحمد حسين صقر
AHMAD HUSSEIN SAKR

خطب الجمعة

Friday Khutab

أحمد حسين صقر
Ahmad H. Sakr

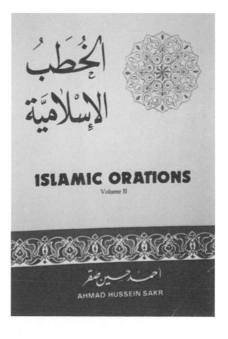

الخُطب
الإسلاميّة

ISLAMIC ORATIONS
Volume II

أحمد حسين صقر
AHMAD HUSSEIN SAKR

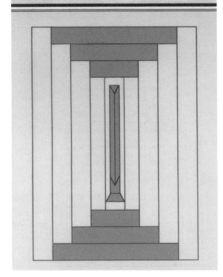

LIFE, DEATH AND THE LIFE AFTER

الخِـنزيـر ..

PORK

POSSIBLE REASONS FOR ITS PROHIBITION

by

Ahmad H. Sakr
Professor of Biochemistry and Nutrition

MATRIMONIAL EDUCATION IN ISLAM

And among His Signs
Is this, that He created
For you mates from among
Yourselves, that ye may
Dwell in tranquility with them,
And He has put love
And mercy between your (hearts):
Verily in that are Signs
For those who reflect.

Qur'an (30:21)

Ahmad H. Sakr, Ph.D.

THE GOLDEN BOOK OF ISLAMIC LISTS

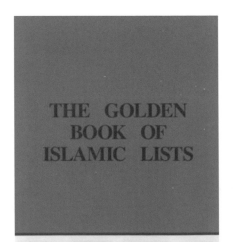

Ahmad H. Sakr, Ph.D.

Farewell Khutbah of The Prophet ﷺ

Its Universal Values

AL-JINN

الجن الجن الجن الجن الجن الجن الجن الجن الجن
الجن الجن الجن الجن الجن الجن الجن الجن الجن
الجن الجن الجن الجن الجن الجن الجن الجن الجن
الجن الجن الجن الجن الجن الجن الجن الجن الجن
الجن الجن الجن الجن الجن الجن الجن الجن الجن

الجن

الجن الجن الجن الجن الجن الجن الجن الجن الجن
الجن الجن الجن الجن الجن الجن الجن الجن الجن
الجن الجن الجن الجن الجن الجن الجن الجن الجن
الجن الجن الجن الجن الجن الجن الجن الجن الجن
الجن الجن الجن الجن الجن الجن الجن الجن الجن
الجن الجن الجن الجن الجن الجن الجن الجن الجن

KHUTAB AL-MASJID

خطب المسجد

قُلْ أَمَرَ رَبِّي بِالْقِسْطِ وَأَقِيمُوا وُجُوهَكُمْ عِندَ كُلِّ مَسْجِدٍ
وَادْعُوهُ مُخْلِصِينَ لَهُ الدِّينَ كَمَا بَدَأَكُمْ تَعُودُونَ ۝

AHMAD H. SAKR, Ph.D.

A
Muslim Guide
to Food
Ingredients

AHMAD H. SAKR, Ph.D.
Professor of Nutritional Biochemistry

ISLAMIC FUNDAMENTALISM

KARM B. AKHTAR, Ph.D.
AHMAD H. SAKR, Ph.D.

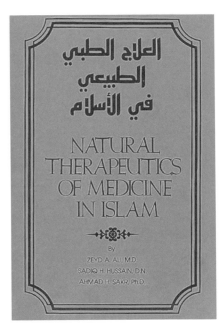

العلاج الطبي
الطبيعي
في الأسلام

NATURAL THERAPEUTICS OF MEDICINE IN ISLAM

By
ZEYD A. ALI, M.D.
SADIQ H. HUSSAIN, D.N.
AHMAD H. SAKR, Ph.D.

GUIDELINES
OF EMPLOYMENT
BY
MUSLIM COMMUNITIES

BY
AHMAD H. SAKR, Ph.D.
&
SAMIR A. ARAFEH, Ph.D.

FASTING
Regulations and Practices

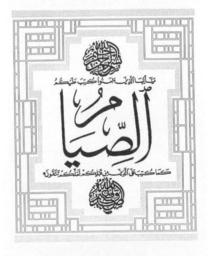

Ahmad H. Sakr, Ph.D.

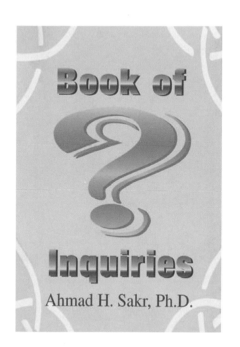

Book of ? Inquiries

Ahmad H. Sakr, Ph.D.

SUJOOD السجود

PROSTRATION

سُبْحَانَ رَبِّيَ الْأَعْلَى

Highly glorified is my Lord, the Most High; and Praise be to Him.

Ahmad H. Sakr

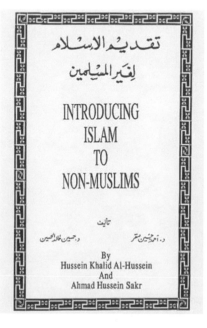

تقديم الاسلام لغَيْر المسلمين

INTRODUCING ISLAM TO NON-MUSLIMS

تأليف

د. حسين خالد الحسين   د. أحمد حسين سقر

By
Hussein Khalid Al-Hussein
And
Ahmad Hussein Sakr

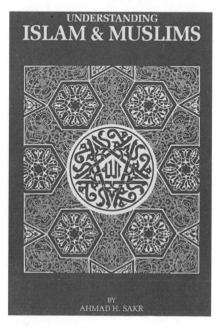

UNDERSTANDING ISLAM & MUSLIMS

BY
AHMAD H. SAKR

Death
&
Dying

Ahmad H. Sakr, Ph.D.

ISLAM & MUSLIMS

Myth
or
Reality

• Ahmad H. Sakr •

ISLAMIC
AWARENESS

AHMAD H. SAKR, Ph.D.

MUSLIMS AND NON-MUSLIMS
FACE TO FACE

AHMAD H. SAKR   Ph.D.

دَلِيلُ
خُطَبِ الجُمُعَة

*A Manual of
Friday Khutab*

تأليف
أحمد حسين صقر
By
Ahmad Hussein Sakr, Ph.D.

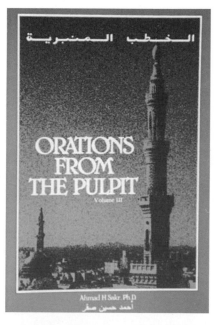

الخطب المنبرية

ORATIONS
FROM
THE PULPIT
Volume III

Ahmad H Sakr, Ph.D.
أحمد حسين صقر

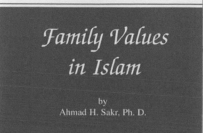

*Family Values
in Islam*

by
Ahmad H. Sakr, Ph. D.

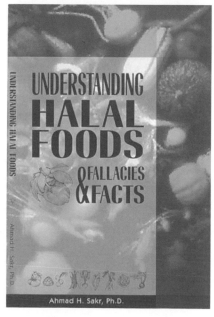

UNDERSTANDING
HALAL
FOODS
& FALLACIES
& FACTS

Ahmad H. Sakr, Ph.D.

Social Services & Counseling

Ahmad H. Sakr, Ph.D.

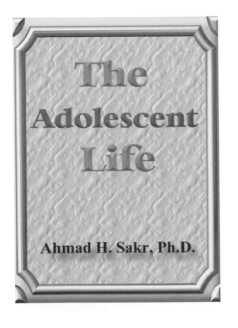

The Adolescent Life

Ahmad H. Sakr, Ph.D.

Gelatin

Ahmad H. Sakr, Ph.D.

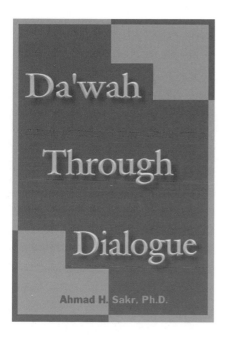

Da'wah
Through
Dialogue

Ahmad H. Sakr, Ph.D.

Feasts
Festivities
Holidays
&

Ahmad H. Sakr, Ph.D.

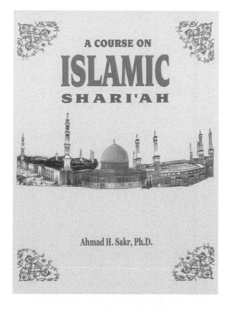

A COURSE ON
ISLAMIC
SHARI'AH

Ahmad H. Sakr, Ph.D.

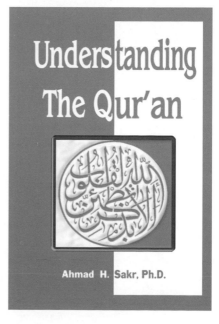

Understanding
The Qur'an

Ahmad H. Sakr, Ph.D.

Themes of the Qur'an

By

Ahmad H. Sakr, Ph.D.

HOW TO PERFORM
HAJJ & UMRAH
(STEP BY STEP)

- Day to Day Hajj Rites (A Flow Chart Approach)
- Useful Tips for Pilgrims (prior, during and after Hajj-trip)
- Comprehesive selected Du'aa's
- Significance of Hajj related subjects

BY
DR. AHMAD H. SAKR &
MASOUD NASSIMI

Book Of Knowledge

Ahmad H. Sakr, Ph.D.

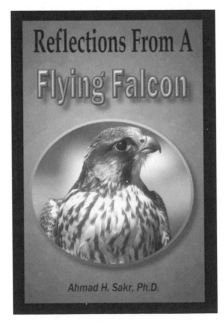

Reflections From A
Flying Falcon

Ahmad H. Sakr, Ph.D.

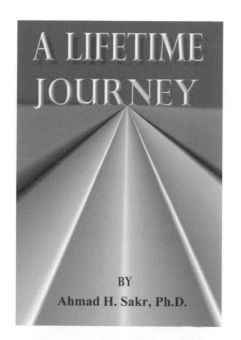

A LIFETIME JOURNEY

BY
Ahmad H. Sakr, Ph.D.

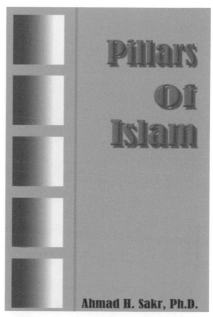

Pillars Of Islam

Ahmad H. Sakr, Ph.D.

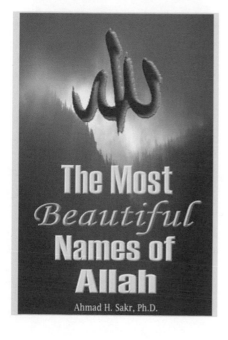

The Most *Beautiful* Names of Allah

Ahmad H. Sakr, Ph.D.

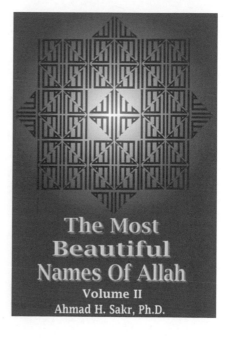

The Most Beautiful Names Of Allah
Volume II
Ahmad H. Sakr, Ph.D.

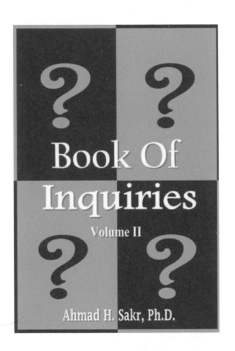

Book Of
Inquiries
Volume II

Ahmad H. Sakr, Ph.D.

Book Of
HEALING

Ahmad H. Sakr, Ph.D.

About Prophet
Muhammad ﷺ

• Ahmad H. Sakr, Ph.D. •

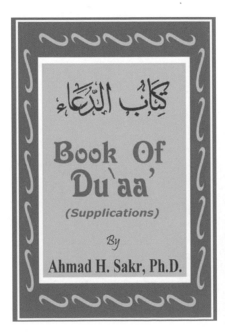

كِتَابُ الدُّعَاءِ

Book Of
Du'aa'
(Supplications)

By

Ahmad H. Sakr, Ph.D.

Book Of Wisdom

كِتَابُ الحِكمَة

AHMAD H. SAKR, PH.D.